Modern Devil's Advocacy

Modern Devil's Advocacy

Disrupt Groupthink, Build Stronger Plans, and Achieve Better Results

Robert Koshinskie

BEP

BUSINESS EXPERT PRESS

Leader in applied, concise business books

Modern Devil's Advocacy:
Disrupt Groupthink, Build Stronger Plans, and Achieve Better Results

Copyright © Business Expert Press, LLC, 2022.

Cover design by Divya Pidaparti

Interior design by Exeter Premedia Services Private Ltd., Chennai, India

First published in 2021 by
Business Expert Press, LLC
222 East 46th Street, New York, NY 10017
www.businessexpertpress.com

ISBN-13: 978-1-63742-175-8 (paperback)
ISBN-13: 978-1-63742-176-5 (e-book)

Business Expert Press Entrepreneurship and Small Business Management Collection

Collection ISSN: 1946-5653 (print)
Collection ISSN: 1946-5661 (electronic)

First edition: 2021

10 9 8 7 6 5 4 3 2 1

For my wife, Diane,
partner, caregiver, artist,
a true alchemist.

Description

In December 1941, shortly after the devastating attack by the Imperial Japanese Navy Air Service on the U.S. naval base at Pearl Harbor in Honolulu, the headquarters of General Douglas MacArthur was warned that a similar attack on his forces in the Philippines may occur. The warning was essentially ignored and ensuing Japanese attacks over the next several days decimated MacArthur's air support, resulting in catastrophic losses and a surrender of U.S. military forces.[1] In 2018, after the start-up biotechnology company, Theranos had achieved a market value of over $9 billion in just 5 years' time, the enterprise crashed into bankruptcy and felony charges of conspiracy and wire fraud against its celebrity founder, Elizabeth Holmes. This spectacular failure was due, in large part, to powerful supporters of the firm who didn't believe in dissenting voices, who challenged the dubious claims and questionable operations of Theranos leadership.

Authoritarian decisions and majority opinions like the earlier examples can lead to disastrous results. How might things have turned out differently in these examples if decision makers had sought out and seriously considered thoughtful, dissenting opinions? How might you avoid failure and achieve better outcomes in your daily business and personal decisions?

Modern Devil's Advocacy is a form of *challenge analysis* that's intended to help overcome our human bias and fallacious reasoning, disrupt groupthink, and achieve better outcomes. By creating a strong counter case to a decision, modern Devil's Advocates can help the original decision makers see potential weaknesses in their assumptions, beliefs, and judgments.

The premise of this book is that practically anyone from the CEO to the newly minted manager can and should think and act like a modern Devil's Advocate. This book discusses the origin of modern Devil's Advocacy, why the practice is needed today, and how to apply modern Devil's Advocacy in any setting. If you want to learn how to constructively challenge the judgments that you and others make to achieve better outcomes, then this book is for you.

Keywords

devil's advocacy; devil's advocate; project management; business analysis; best practice; process improvement; decision making; critical thinking; systems thinking; logical argument; cognitive bias; logical fallacy; groupthink; lean start-up; agile; structured analytic technique; red team; red hat

Contents

Testimonials

"Robert Koshinskie makes a compelling case for the devil's advocate and offers practical advice for those brave enough to play that important role in their organization. This sort of applied critical thinking is exactly what companies need more of if they are to not only thrive, but survive, in today's complex and rapidly changing world."—**Bryce G. Hoffman, President, Red Team Thinking LLC, author of** ***Red Teaming: How Your Business Can Conquer the Competition by Challenging Everything***

"Succinctly explains modern Devil's Advocacy and provides clear guidelines on how to conduct a useful challenge analysis. A fantastic book that provides a great deal of value to the reader."—**Theodore Kalmbach, Chief Strategy Officer, BNNano, Inc.**

"As a former participant in the NSF I-Corps Program, I really enjoyed Robert Koshinskie's guidance on how to apply modern Devil's Advocacy in daily practice. His book will be useful to industry mentors, graduate researchers, and faculty members who are involved in technology transfer efforts, including the I-Corps Program."—**Maryam Rahmaniheris, PhD, Upstream Product Manager, Spacelabs Healthcare**

Acknowledgments

Thanks to those who gave their valuable time to review and comment on the material for this book.

Bryce Hoffman, president of Red Team Thinking LLC. In 2015, Hoffman became the first civilian to graduate from the U.S. Army's Red Team Leader Program at the University of Foreign Military and Cultural Studies at Fort Leavenworth, Kansas. Hoffman is a lecturer at U.C. Berkeley's Haas School of Business and writes a column on leadership and business culture for Forbes.com. Hoffman appears regularly on television and radio shows in the United States and around the world, including the BBC, NPR, CNN, Fox Business, and Bloomberg.

Theodore Kalmbach, chief strategy officer with the advanced materials firm, BNNano. Prior to his current position, Kalmbach held a variety of positions where challenge analysis was critical, including as a diplomat for the U.S. Department of State, an analyst for the Institute for Defense Analyses (where he advised the Pentagon on counterinsurgency strategy), and a strategy consultant for Accenture in Munich and Berlin.

Maryam Rahmaniheris, PhD whose various research includes the design and evaluation of integrated emergency medical assist systems to mitigate preventable medical errors. Dr. Rahmaniheris was also a participant in the National Science Foundation Innovation Corps Program (NSF I-Corps) which I discuss later in this book.

Rosemary Tracy, marketing/advertising professional and entrepreneur, with a focus in Business and Management. Rosemary is a former director of Colangelo Synergy Marketing and vice president of G2 Marketing/Subsidiary of Grey Advertising (formerly J. Brown LMC).

Thanks also to those who reviewed the material of my earlier work, excerpts of which appear in this book. Kristan Wheaton, professor of Strategic Futures, U.S. Army War College. David Johnson, former president and current senior advisor to Laerdal Medical Corporation. Linda Hurwitz, entrepreneur, advisor, and coach to CEOs and business owners. Gene Bellinger, organizational theorist in systems thinking and knowledge management. Thomas Dyar, specialist in machine learning and artificial intelligence and former manager for External Innovation & Data Science at Becton Dickinson. Tracie Coletto, former senior field marketing manager for Philips Healthcare. Thomas Hogan, entrepreneur, chief financial officer, general manager, old friend, and advisor.

Finally, thanks to the BEP editorial and production team for their guidance and work to produce the book that you now hold: Scott Isenberg, Scott Shane, Charlene Kronstedt, Melissa Yeager, Divya Pidaparti. Thanks, too, to Gunabala Saladi and the team at Exeter Premedia Services.

Introduction

The book that you are now holding discusses modern Devil's Advocacy and presents a view that is likely at odds with your understanding of the term. As I'll explain in the pages ahead, modern Devil's Advocacy is not about role-playing or yet another stepwise process or best practice that claims to reliably lead to the *right* answer. A balance of intuition and analysis, modern Devil's Advocacy is about applying a usefully skeptical point of view and behaviors that can help address our cognitive bias and fallacious reasoning. The guidance I offer should not be considered a new and improved dogma, but a foundational skill required for other analyses and decision making.

The concepts discussed in this book do not require that you have a background or expertise in business, science, or any other domain. *Modern Devil's Advocacy* is not limited to any specific persona and can be practiced by anyone regardless of their age, experience, training, gender, and so on. I use gender-based pronouns in the book material (he, she, his, and hers) randomly so the content is inclusive—no other meaning should be attributed to the use of these pronouns. Practically anyone from the CEO to the new hire can become a modern Devil's Advocate if they have the desire to do so. If you practice modern Devil's Advocacy, then you are a modern Devil's Advocate.

I've organized this book into two sections. Section I offers a brief history of Devil's Advocacy, discusses the many challenges to decision making in today's complex world, and suggests how the practice of modern Devil's Advocacy can help improve judgments. Section II provides guidance in the practice of modern Devil's Advocacy that can be applied to practically any situation, and I include an example of the unofficial role that modern Devil's Advocacy serves in the popular *lean start-up*[1] approach. I hope that you find the journey ahead interesting and informative, and that you consider embracing the daily practice of modern Devil's Advocacy.

SECTION I

The Case for Modern Devil's Advocacy

The term *Devil's Advocate* is very common these days. While writing this book, I ran a Google search that returned about three million instances of the term. Unfortunately, Devil's Advocacy and the role of a modern Devil's Advocate are widely misunderstood. Very often, Devil's Advocacy is reduced to either a simple opinion offered by a friend or business associate, or as a conveniently superficial means to attack another person's character. Consequently, many may believe that they are acting as a modern Devil's Advocate or are the unfortunate target of Devil's Advocate's personal attack. In this first section of the book, I'll provide an overview of modern Devil's Advocacy to dispel common misinterpretations of the practice, to explore the need to regularly challenge our assumptions and judgments, and to understand the usefulness that modern Devil's Advocacy offers.

A Very Brief History of Devil's Advocacy

Devil's Advocacy is a very old idea that serves as a model for the modern Devil's Advocacy discussed in this book. The concept of Devil's Advocacy originated in the Roman Catholic Church around 1381 AD and was institutionalized as a Church practice a couple of hundred years later.[1] The purpose of this practice was to investigate popular candidates for whom sainthood was proposed. The men who were tasked to conduct these investigations held the official title of *Promotor of the Faith*. Working *against* a person's sainthood, however, these individuals were commonly referred to as the *Devil's Advocate*.

The role of the original Devil's Advocate emerged from a decision in the 1630s by the Church leadership to have more uniform standards when considering a proposed candidate for sainthood. Prior to the appearance of the Devil's Advocate, local clergy and parishioners might revere any popular individual as a saint. For example, "In rural France, St. Guinefort was venerated as the protector of infants after he saved his master's baby from a snakebite. St. Guinefort was a dog."[2] Devil's Advocates were key participants in the Church's move toward a laws-based approach to sainthood that was similar to the Courts of the Inquisition and is why both endeavors shared the structure of a trial (i.e., witnesses, depositions, evidence).[3]

By the 20th century, the duties of the Church's Devil's Advocate included the prevention of any "rash decisions concerning miracles or virtues of the candidates" and "to suggest natural explanations for alleged miracles, and even to bring forward human and selfish motives for deeds that have been accounted heroic virtues."[4] You may find it interesting that Pope John Paul II essentially eliminated the role of the Devil's Advocate in the 1980s, a decision that has opened the floodgates to sainthood. According to the *U.S. Catholic Magazine*, "Revisions to the canonization process in 1983 ensured we will see more saints in the future … John Paul II canonized more saints than the popes from the previous 500 years combined."[5] Perhaps, we'll see more canine saints in the coming years?

This book discusses modern, secular Devil's Advocacy, which is unrelated to its religious origin. However, the purpose of modern Devil's Advocacy is still to challenge the decision-making process and thereby help arrive at better decisions—absent the need for miraculous claims! Former CIA intelligence analysts Richards Heuer and Randolph Pherson define modern Devil's Advocacy as:

> A process for critiquing a proposed analytic judgement, plan, or decision, usually by a single analyst not previously involved in the deliberations that led to the proposed judgment, plan, or decision … The Devil's Advocate is charged with challenging the proposed judgment by building the strongest possible case against it. There is no prescribed procedure.[6]

Devil's Advocacy is one of over 45 techniques that Heuer and Pherson include in their book *Structured Analytic Techniques for Intelligence*

Analysis, and it is the foundation for many other techniques, including Red Hat Analysis and Red Team Analysis.[7] Certainly, the modern Devil's Advocate should explore, learn, and apply a variety of techniques that are appropriate and useful for different situations. I'm focusing solely on Devil's Advocacy in this book rather than the many other methods for three main reasons.

1. Devil's Advocacy requires an inquisitive mind and active thinking skills, both of which are basic behaviors in all analytic techniques and decision making.
2. Devil's Advocacy typically involves a single analyst who can help provide a useful challenge without requiring a large team and other precious resources.
3. Devil's Advocacy can help disrupt the tendency for a group of reasonable people to make unreasonable or non-optimal decisions in order to maintain harmony (i.e., groupthink[8]) and may help overcome the inhibiting influence that others have on our inclination to act when important decisions need to be made (i.e., the bystander effect[9,10]).

Modern Devil's Advocates pursue the habits of a good analytic thinker as itemized by Heuer and Pherson:

- Know when to challenge key assumptions (usually far more often than you think, according to Heuer and Pherson)
- Consider alternative explanations or hypotheses for all events
- Look for inconsistent data that provides sufficient justification to quickly discard a candidate hypothesis
- Focus on the key drivers that best explain what has occurred or what is about to happen
- Anticipate the client's needs and understand the overarching context within which the analysis is being done

Modern Devil's Advocacy is neither a simple opinion nor a means of mounting a personal attack on another person, rather it is a thoughtful practice that is intended to offer useful analysis and achieve better outcomes.

Modern Devil's Advocates Aren't Cynics

You may have the impression that modern Devil's Advocates are by nature disagreeable *cynics*, faultfinding critics who have an ill-natured inclination to point to insignificant shortcomings and raise annoying objections.[11] Modern Devil's Advocacy, however, isn't about questioning plain facts or proposing far-out conspiracy theories. Arguing that 2 plus 2 doesn't equal 4 or asserting that alien lizards rule us are not the kinds of challenges that modern Devil's Advocacy is intended to make.[12]

Unlike cynics and so-called *conspiracy theorists*, modern Devil's Advocates seek practical and useful alternative perspectives to a majority view. This contrarian posture places modern Devil's Advocates squarely into the camp of *skeptics*, adherents or advocates of doubt who question the truthfulness of claims.[13] There are many forms of skeptics ranging from those who believe that nothing can ever be known or believed to those who view skeptical inquiry as an essential, positive, and constructive tool in all facets of our lives. The modern Devil's Advocate rejects the former pessimistic view in favor of the latter constructive stance.

The late philosopher, Paul Kurtz, specifically noted that "Skeptical inquirers are not negative skeptics, naysayers, debunkers, or nihilists," and he offered a set of principles for what has been called *exuberant skepticism*.[14] Following are elements of Kurtz's principles, which I've aligned to the behaviors of a modern Devil's Advocate:

- Applies skepticism to all areas of human endeavor, including everyday life, to achieve positive ends
- Recognizes that critical thinking is an inherent component of skeptical inquiry
- Seeks "clarity rather than obfuscation, lucid meaning in place of confusion"
- Acknowledges the benefits of the theoretical but seeks to objectively test claims with "facts, not suppositions … logical inference and deduction, not faith or intuition"[15]
- Questions absolute dogmas and creeds and believes in "inquiry rather than authority, reason in the place of custom"

The benefits of skeptical inquiry are not simply the opinions of philosophers like Kurtz and can be seen at work in the real world. The field of financial auditing, for example, relies on *professional skepticism* which has been described as "... an attitude that includes a questioning mind and a critical assessment of audit evidence ... regardless of any past experience with the entity and regardless of the auditor's belief about management's honesty and integrity."[16]

Note that the statement above does not presume intentional fraud, rather professional skepticism is neutral and "... relates to the integrity and good faith of the auditor who does not assume honesty or dishonesty on the part of the audit client."[17] Professional skepticism can be further categorized as either *evidence skepticism* or *judgment skepticism*. As the names indicate, the first type challenges the facts, while the second type questions decision making. Financial auditors provided the following two examples of these different forms of skepticism that may be similar to your own experiences:[18]

- **Evidence skepticism**: "During my first busy season, I took the word of the HR dept regarding headcounts of one of my client's subsidiaries and it turned out to be wrong."
- **Judgment skepticism**: "Upon taking on a job that was new to me as a manager I placed more reliance than I should have on the prior team's work. I should have spent more time challenging some of the conclusions and understanding them such that I could own them throughout the audit process."

Of course, the benefits of professional skepticism are also found outside of financial accounting; for example, Dharmesh Shah, founder and CTO at HubSpot has noted that:[19]

- Skeptics can be extremely useful members of a team. They don't just accept ideas, proposals, opinions, or even "facts" as offered—they need to be convinced.
- Skeptics like to look at data. They like to analyze. They like to assess. Skeptics like to weigh and measure and draw their own conclusions.

- Skeptics don't wear rose-colored glasses. Skeptics temper the enthusiasm—often in a good way—of the instantly enthusiastic and in the process often apply a level of analysis and rigor that transforms a good idea into a great idea—and just as important, help recognize bad ideas.

By analyzing a popular judgment, the modern Devil's Advocate can challenge not only the *instantly enthusiastic* to which Shah refers but also the chronically gloomy. This means that the modern Devil's Advocate can help expose weaknesses of a popular pet project *and* reveal strengths of a project that the majority believes is doomed to fail. The modern Devil's Advocate is not invested in a particular position and so is open to creating a counter position to whatever the majority opinion happens to be, regardless her personal view of the majority opinion.

I will be referring to *the* modern Devil's Advocate because it is generally the case that an individual is serving in the role. This reference to a solo practitioner is certainly not meant to imply that only one or a few parties can or should embrace modern Devil's Advocacy in an organization. I feel that it could be immensely helpful to an enterprise if everyone from the CEO to the new hire has a common understanding of the purpose and practice of modern Devil's Advocacy. There may be individuals who are more strongly predisposed to the practice of modern Devil's Advocacy but having many team members who are familiar with modern Devil's Advocacy may benefit the efforts of modern Devil's Advocates.

If you are a CEO or senior manager, then you may worry that a modern Devil's Advocate could create serious logjams through endless debates about the pros and cons of an issue, effectively bringing progress to a halt. I discuss later under *Organizational Dissent and Group Decisions* why dissent can be beneficial in decision making and how to manage dissent while still maintaining forward motion toward objectives.

Finally, perhaps you believe that modern Devil's Advocacy isn't necessary because experienced executives and professional managers like you are already making good assumptions, judgments, and decisions? As we'll explore next, such belief doesn't seem well justified.

Modern Devil's Advocacy Matters Today

You've likely noticed how a majority opinion can lead to very impressive, although sometimes perplexing, outcomes. Popularity can propel an otherwise unremarkable person into a high office or turn a social network blogger into a wealthy and influential celebrity. Such majority support can lead to unwanted and negative outcomes like social unrest and countless hours staring at a smartphone, but life goes on.[20,21] Perhaps, the popular majority opinion is generally a good thing that ought to be protected from examination by modern Devil's Advocacy? Perhaps not.

Consider the case of the Theranos company whose youthful founder, Elizabeth Holmes, attracted broad support for her venture with a baritone-voiced visionary persona that she created. Holmes successfully gained high-profile supporters whose involvement helped her raise millions of dollars of funding for Theranos. Holmes's roster of investors contained many highly regarded individuals, including "Oracle founder Larry Ellison, venture capital firm Draper Fisher Jurvetson, Secretary of Education Betsy DeVos and media mogul Rupert Murdoch."[22] The din from the growing number of fervent Holmes's supporters and the escalating valuation of Theranos seemed to drown out reasoned dissent offered by several notable parties, including:[23]

- Dr. Phyllis Gardner, a Stanford Medical School professor who expressed skepticism about Holmes's concept on technical grounds.
- Theranos Chief Financial Officer Henry Mosley who "was fired after questioning the reliability of its technology and the honesty of the company."
- The chief medical officer of Safeway who questioned "discrepancies in the test results" which didn't dissuade Safeway's CEO.
- Lieutenant Colonel David Shoemaker who "raised concerns about Theranos' regulatory strategy to the FDA" and reportedly revised his position after "battling James Mattis, who was on the Theranos board."[24]

The arc of the Theranos journey peaked at a $9 billion valuation and collapsed under the weight of criminal investigations and indictments of Holmes and her co-founder for conspiracy and wire fraud. If we were seeking an example of a case where dissenting voices should have been heeded, then Theranos is such an example.

Of course, similar consolidation of decision making is going on today. For example, the *Wall Street Journal* has noted that Facebook CEO, Mark Zuckerberg, tends to create an environment that discounts dissent[25] and *The New York Times* reported that Zuckerberg has built a board of directors that favors his decisions:

> Kenneth Chenault, the former chief executive of American Express, suggested creating an independent committee to scrutinize the company's challenges and pose the sort of probing questions the board wasn't used to being asked … Other board disagreements, specifically around political advertising, and the spread of misinformation, always ended with Mr. Zuckerberg's point of view winning out.[26]

I'm not comparing Zuckerberg's intentions and actions to those of Holmes, but perhaps, there are good reasons to be concerned about the consolidation of decision making around one or a few persons, lack of transparency, and the absence of strong dissent?

Modern Devil's Advocacy may also offer benefits outside of the business domain, particularly as a tonic against widely distributed misinformation. From the early appearance of the COVID-19 virus, a host of rumors were spreading as quickly as the pandemic. The following were some of the more popular allegations that were circulating on the Internet: [27]

- It is a bioweapon that was inadvertently or intentionally unleashed. This claim has reportedly been linked to "former Iranian president Mahmoud Ahmadinejad, Chinese Foreign Ministry spokesman Lijian Zhao, and US Sen. Tom Cotton of Arkansas."[28]
- A patented virus as part of a plot involving Microsoft® founder, Bill Gates. Reportedly advanced by conspiracy theorists who

also believe that the U.S. military put Donald Trump into the White House to save the country from pedophilic Satanists.[29]

- Corona® brand of beer has something to do with the virus. Reportedly, "16% of beer drinking Americans were confused about whether Corona beer is related to the coronavirus."[30,31]
- Certain "colloidal silver solutions" are effective cures for the virus, including a tonic promoted by the disgraced televangelist, Jim Bakker,[32] and a "nanosilver toothpaste" promoted by the infamous conspiracy theorist, Alex Jones.[33]

Such peculiar beliefs aren't uncommon and can be difficult to rectify, especially in highly charged situations. During the 2015 and 2016 Zika epidemic in Brazil, even attempts to correct misinformation led to counterintuitive results as investigators reported, "… efforts to counter misperceptions about diseases during epidemics and outbreaks may not always be effective. We find that corrective information not only fails to reduce targeted Zika misperceptions but also reduces the accuracy of other beliefs about the disease."[34]

The failure of active attempts to correct erroneous information is particularly troubling when you consider that little to no such corrective action is taken to confirm the countless claims made daily on social networks. A survey conducted by Harris Poll,[35] for example, revealed how easily misinformation can be spread through social networks, noting that:

- 86 percent of people don't fact check the news they read on social media.
- 79 percent of Americans on social media said they trust at least some of the content shared by friends.
- When Americans read a news article shared by a friend on social media, the most common action they took was to then share it themselves (32 percent). That's an important point because it highlights just how easily news that may be erroneous, misleading, inaccurate, or entirely made up can spread.

Even more troubling, it appears as though when fact-checking is provided, it may do little to change the opinion of those who are misinformed.

Fact-checking might harden strongly held beliefs. Researchers at *The Brookings Institution* looked at the *political informedness* of participants in four categories: [36]

- **Informed**: Those who know a fact and are confident in their knowledge
- **Uninformed**: Those who know that they don't know a fact
- **Misinformed**: Those who believe they know a fact but are mistaken
- **Ambiguously informed**: Those who acknowledge that they are just guessing

After being asked a series of questions, the participants were shown the related fact checks. The fact checks confirmed for the Informed what they already knew and benefitted the Uninformed, Misinformed, and Ambiguously informed. However, the Misinformed benefitted least from the fact check and were *more likely to continue to choose the wrong answer even after reading the fact check*. Further, although a story clearly labeled as a fact check helped readers get the facts right, the fact check label also led people "to become more likely to report that the fact-check was biased."

As examples like those above indicate, it seems that people may be content or predisposed to simply accept and share information that is misleading or false, even when they have a good reason to believe that the information is misleading or false.[37] This counterintuitive behavior opens wide a door for those who wish to spread misleading and false information as a kind of prank or to advance an agenda. Imagine, however, if more individuals embraced the behaviors of a modern Devil's Advocate and took the initiative to employ informed skepticism rather than rushing to pass along information that may be false or misleading. In the book, *Conspiracy Theories and the People Who Believe Them*, conspiracy researcher, Joseph Uscinski, notes that conspiracy theories offer some benefits such as encouraging transparency and fostering a healthy skepticism. Uscinski asks, "If conspiracy theorists do not test establishment truths, who will do it?"[38] My answer to Uscinski's question is, modern Devil's Advocates!

If you are a professional who is well educated and well paid, then you may believe that you are uniquely able to avoid the influence of misinformation and make rational judgments. However, there exists ample evidence that critical thinking skills are sorely lacking even in seasoned professionals. A quick Google search will lead you to a host of articles on the need for better critical thinking skills in our schools and workplaces. The search will also reveal numerous initiatives where schools, government, and private organizations have attempted to close the thinking skills gap. There has been so much activity related to thinking skills that you may wonder how a thinking skills gap could exist. Perhaps, the thinking skills gap problem is so *thorny* that the many prescriptive processes and best practices intended to improve critical thinking skills simply aren't working? Whatever the reasons, the World Economic Forum[39] warns about trouble ahead due in part to poor skills like critical thinking and problem solving: [40]

- By 2022, no less than 54 percent of all employees will require significant reskilling and upskilling.
- Skills continuing to grow in prominence by 2022 include analytical thinking and innovation as well as active learning and learning strategies.
- Proficiency in new technologies is only one part of the 2022 skills equation; however, as *human* skills such as creativity, originality and initiative, critical thinking, persuasion, and negotiation will likewise retain or increase their value, as will attention to detail, resilience, flexibility, and complex problem solving.
- Emotional intelligence, leadership, and social influence, as well as service orientation, also see an outsized increase in demand relative to their current prominence.

The Forum Report observes that industries appear to limit their skills training for employees to today's roles rather than to future skills needs and advises that industries should actively address future skills and close the gap, to become *learning organizations*.[41] The Forum Report also advises workers to "take personal responsibility" for their "lifelong learning and career development," adding that "many individuals will need to be supported through periods of job transition and phases of retraining and upskilling by governments and employers." The report suggests that a combination of personal responsibility and worker support could lead to voluntary skills upgrade under some form of a "universal lifelong learning fund" for individuals to use as needed. These kinds of personal development initiatives could create fertile ground to promote and expand the practice of modern Devil's Advocacy.

Another perspective on the importance of strong thinking skills was offered in the article *Good Data Won't Guarantee Good Decisions*.[42] The authors of the article reported their findings from an evaluation that included 5,000 employees at 22 global companies and how those employees made sense of data that was available to them. The evaluation sorted employees into three distinct groups:

1. **Unquestioning empiricists** who trust analysis over judgment
2. **Visceral decision makers** who go exclusively with their gut
3. **Informed skeptics** who the authors identified as those "employees best equipped to make good decisions—effectively balance judgment and analysis, possess strong analytic skills, and listen to others' opinions but are willing to dissent"

The authors concluded that the Informed skeptics were "the kind of data-savvy workers every company should try to cultivate" because these workers had higher performance. The authors noted, however, that "only 38% of employees, and 50% of senior managers, fall into this group." This finding complements the Forum Report view that industries and workers are facing a significant gap in skills and behaviors that can hinder productivity.

The problems created by poor thinking skills and weak analysis are recognized at the highest levels of business organizations. In the article, *The Case for Behavioral Strategy*, the authors recount a survey that was conducted with 2,207 executives, which revealed that: [43]

- Only 28 percent of respondents said that the quality of strategic decisions in their companies was generally good.
- 60 percent thought that bad decisions were about as frequent as good ones.
- 12 percent thought good decisions were altogether infrequent.

- Cognitive biases affect the most important strategic decisions made by the smartest managers in the best companies.
- Mergers routinely fail to deliver the expected synergies and strategic plans often ignore competitive responses.
- Large investment projects are over budget and over time—over and over again.

A similar perspective on the need for soft skills is provided in the 2019 IBM Institute for Business Value report entitled, *The Enterprise Guide to Closing the Skills Gap* that included the following findings:[44]

- Digital skills remain vital; however, executives tell us soft skills have surpassed them in importance.
- Executives recognize the skills gap. They know it's both real and problematic. But most of their organizations don't appear to be actively or effectively tackling the issue.
- Not surprisingly, different management styles are required as well—ones that encourage an agile work environment that includes autonomous decision making, work product iteration, experimentation, peer-to-peer coaching, and flexible team structures.
- IBM Chairman Ginni Rometty coined the term *new collar*—"jobs [that] emphasize academic and technical skills, along with professional competencies such as critical thinking, collaboration, and communication."

Apparently, business leaders are unable to correct poor decision-making skills in their organizations of which they are well aware. This is a particularly important issue because our learning institutions may not be adequately addressing the thinking skills gap either. In 2019, *The Global Learner Survey*[45] was completed by over 11,000 people between 16 and 70 years of age who were located around the world. The findings from the survey included the following insights:

- Almost half of those in the United States, UK, Australia, Canada, and Europe don't think that higher education prepared them for their career.

- Workers everywhere want skills that machines, and artificial intelligence (AI) can't yet compete with—critical thinking, problem solving, and creativity. Educational institutions aren't yet meeting this need.
- 70 percent of people agree that colleges and universities care more about their reputation than educating students.
- 74 percent of respondents agree that colleges and universities focus too much on young students and should offer better options for working adults.

Skills development, however, requires moving from theory to daily practice. In the paper *Teaching Critical Thinking: Some Lessons from Cognitive Science*, the author observed:

> For students to improve, they must engage in critical thinking itself. It is not enough to learn about critical thinking. Many college professors seem unaware of this point: they teach a course on the theory of critical thinking and assume that their students will end up better critical thinkers. Other teachers make a dissimilar mistake: They expose their students to examples of good critical thinking (for example, having them read articles by professional philosophers), hoping that students will learn by imitation. These strategies are about as effective as working on your tennis by watching Wimbledon. Unless the students are actively doing the thinking themselves, they will never improve.[46]

In another paper, *What Our Students Have Taught Us About Critical Thinking*, the authors note, "Critical thinking is not a process used only occasionally, but a complete way of thinking. Making it a basis of every course could facilitate more questioning attitudes, logical thinking, and clearer communication by students and teachers alike."[47] These kinds of regular and active practices to reinforce critical thinking skills could be beneficial to businesses that strive to be learning organizations "… where people continually expand their capacity to create the results they truly desire, where new and expansive patterns of thinking are nurtured, where collective aspiration is set free, and where people are continually learning to see the whole together."[48]

Beyond the benefits to business, improved thinking skills may also offer personal benefits. According to the paper, *Predicting Real-world Outcomes*, researchers found that critical thinking ability is a better predictor of life events than is intelligence.[49] The authors concluded, "There is ample evidence that critical thinking can be taught, so there is hope that teaching critical thinking skills might prevent the occurrence of negative life events. We advocate for critical thinking instruction as a way to create a better future for everyone."[50]

The lack of thinking skills training in our education systems and businesses raises an important question. If neither our educational systems nor businesses are adequately addressing decision-making skills, then is our world trapped in a reinforcing loop that is increasing the poor analyses and judgments? To make matters worse, we often try to *fix* the problem of poor thinking skills through prescriptive processes and best practices that may have little or no evidence of usefulness. As we'll explore next, we tend to operate on simplified, subjective, and automatic perspectives that favor comforting narratives but can (and do) easily mislead us every day.

Our Mind's Eye Misleads Us

The term *mind's eye* refers to the way that we imagine or picture something in our thoughts, as in the way that you remember the face of an old friend. Initially, your mental picture may seem complete to you, but when you meet your friend, you note additional information like eye color or presence of a mole. Likewise, we imagine various *mental models*, those simplified representations of the way the world works that we hold in our minds and use continuously, albeit unconsciously. In that sense, mental models are a figment of our imagination and not a particularly accurate version of the real world in which we operate.

An historical example of a mental model is the idea of the atom that physicist William Thomson (aka Lord Kelvin) proposed around 1900.[51]

Thomson's model envisioned atoms as "uniform spheres of positively charged matter in which electrons are embedded"—a description that led some to compare Thomson's model to plum pudding. While this analogy is useful to quickly form a mental image that conveys Thomson's general idea, we (presumably) understand that's where the usefulness ends and shouldn't further imagine other pudding-like characteristics of the atom such as taste and texture. Models like Thomson's are modified or abandoned when they are found lacking and are replaced by other models that offer a better explanation.

We also use mental models to interpret actions that we and others take, automatically considering possible causes and effects of those actions. Our mental models can distort reality through our personal beliefs, cognitive biases, and fallacious reasoning. Consequently, we will do well to remember two popular cautions about mental models (italics are mine):

- "A map is not the territory it represents, but, if correct, it has a similar structure to the territory, which accounts for its *usefulness*," Alfred Korzybski, scientist, and philosopher.[52]
- "All models are wrong, but some are *useful*," George E.P. Box, statistician.[53]

Note that both preceding warnings refer to the *usefulness* of models not because they are *right* but because they may represent the world just well enough to provide us with practical insight and understanding. Upon his death, *The New York Times* noted Korzybski's view that "men did not properly evaluate the world they talked about … spoke before observing and then reacted to their own remarks as if they were fact itself."[54] The modern Devil's Advocate certainly should avoid emulating those comforting, self-confirming kinds of behaviors and help others to do the same.

To share our mental models with others, we can express them as formal, written, or diagrammed *processes*, that is, "a series of actions or operations."[55] Processes based on our mental models may be as simple as a map that you sketch to show someone how to get to your house or a more formal set of steps to achieve an outcome shown as follows:

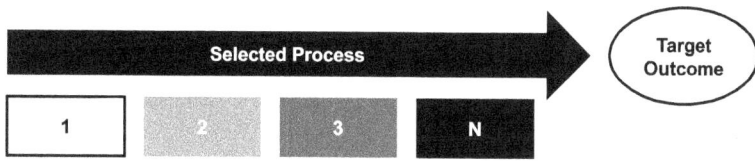

Figure 1.1 A simple formal process

Many processes seem to be commonsense, and their obviousness can entice us to accept them as factual based on their face value. By simply accepting a process, however, we can unintentionally contribute to *groupthink*, "a pattern of thought characterized by self-deception, forced manufacture of consent, and conformity to group values and ethics." [56,57] Simple models can create distortion by oversimplification that misleads us to inappropriately apply the model to situations where it does not apply. Consider how the work of psychiatrist Elisabeth Kübler-Ross was widely misconstrued after the publication of her seminal book, *On Death and Dying*.

Reportedly,[58] Kübler-Ross's goal was to start a conversation about how to improve care for terminally ill patients. In her book, Kübler-Ross described in detail five stages of emotion experienced by such patients: denial, anger, bargaining, depression, and acceptance. Apparently, "The five stages took on a life of their own. They were used to train doctors and therapists, passed on to patients and their families." However, there were never only five stages, and everyone didn't go through stages in a specific order, rather Kübler-Ross's model was intended to be a "loose framework." George Bonanno, professor of clinical psychology, observed that "People who don't go through these stages—and as far as I can tell that's most people—can be led to believe that they are grieving incorrectly." While we may find linear, stepwise models of our world comforting, such a view can also obscure the fact that straightforward and certain paths are not necessarily (or reasonably) assured.[59]

Because our formal processes emerge from our mental models, our formal processes can offer useful insights for modern Devil's Advocacy work. By examining formal processes, the modern Devil's Advocate may better understand and challenge the underlying facts, assumptions, beliefs, premises, and judgments of those who created or follow a process.

Let's now explore just a few of the many factors that can influence our mental models and our attempts to apply those simple models in the real world. I've selected the following eight factors because I've regularly encountered them in the business setting:

Figure 1.2 *Factors influencing mental models' creation and application*

Trailing Processes

Many formal processes are used in businesses out of belief that they provide a reliable path to a desired outcome. The mental model behind these processes is much like a map of a well-marked hiking path that guides us from the trail head to a beautiful outlook point. As long as we carefully follow the map and remain on the marked trail, we have high confidence that we won't get lost along the way. I refer to these kinds of proven process as *trailing* because we are following in the footsteps of many others who walked a path to a successful outcome.

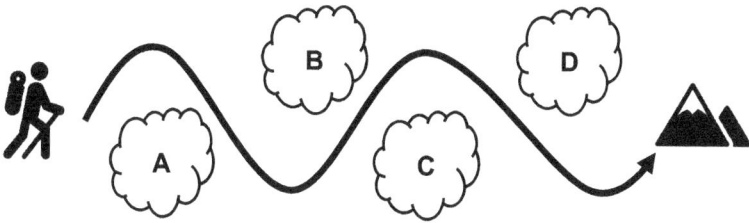

Figure 1.3 A well-marked hiking trail

Business operations like the following customer order process diagram are also examples of the trailing process type. These kinds of processes can be enforced by software-driven systems to help ensure that all of the necessary steps are completed in the right order to properly receive an order, check the customer's credit, accept payment, and ship the product in a timely fashion.

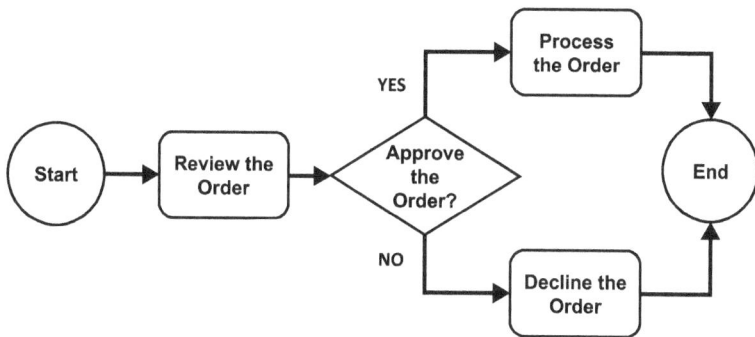

Figure 1.4 A simple order review and approval process

There are many other, similar activities in our daily lives where step-wise trailing processes can be remarkably effective. Preflight checklists, for example, are used by pilots before takeoff to help ensure that no critical preparation tasks are overlooked.[60] Similarly, pre-surgery checklists are used by health care professionals to avoid errors and reduce patient morbidity and mortality.[61]

In addition to the simple kinds of trailing processes described, more advanced frameworks of trailing processes have proven to be very effective. Six Sigma,[62] for example, includes a variety of techniques and tools that can greatly reduce the causes of defects and variability in manufacturing and thereby increase quality and reduce costs. So useful are trailing processes, however, that we may attempt to apply them even when the process may not be appropriate or useful.

For example, referring to the *define, measure, analyze, improve, control (DMAIC) process* within Six Sigma, a certified Six Sigma Black Belt practitioner observed, "… in some situations, DMAIC is just the wrong approach to a business problem, and when that is the case proceeding with a project can worsen the situation rather than fixing it, or at best delay a proper solution."[63] This same Black Belt offered several warning signs that DMAIC may not be appropriate for a project, including:

- The project sponsor or Six Sigma director cannot clearly state the problem that the project was chartered to solve.
- There is no way to obtain sufficient data to evaluate process performance and customer satisfaction.
- The solution to a problem is already clear, but leaders are hesitant to implement it for political or similar reasons—to essentially put the burden on someone else.
- The process or organization is undergoing such dramatic changes that a DMAIC project would not be effective.

Useful trailing processes are similar, in that they can be shown to be reliable when properly applied. Metrics can be established and monitored to demonstrate causality between the actions taken and the outcomes achieved in a useful trailing process. Handwashing procedures, for example, have been shown to reduce the number of people who get sick with diarrhea by 23–40 percent, respiratory illnesses like colds by 16–21 percent, and absenteeism due to gastrointestinal illness in schoolchildren by 29–57 percent.[64]

By contrast, formal business processes in areas like marketing, project management, and business analysis lack the means to test their reliability. Absent the rigor of objective analytical methods, we are simply speculating about causes of success and failure and may reinforce our preconceived and positive opinion of a favored process. Consequently, we typically employ trailing business processes with confidence that our journey will be as straightforward as following a map of a well-marked hiking trail. High confidence in popular but unproven business processes, however, is likely unfounded due to *equifinality* and *multifinality*.

Equifinality and Multifinality

It used to be said that *all roads lead to Rome*, which was likely true of ancient times in Italy when Rome was essentially at the center of that part of the world. Conversely, you could start in Rome and end up in a variety of other destinations. The same many-to-one and one-to-many relationships are also true for our formal business processes.

Simply stated, *equifinality* is when the same outcome occurs even when starting with different initial conditions and taking different actions (i.e., all roads lead to Rome). *Multifinality* is when a given set of initial conditions and prescribed actions lead to different outcomes (i.e., starting from Rome and ending up in a town that you wanted to avoid).[65] Referring to the following diagram, we can contemplate the effects of equifinality and multifinality in business:

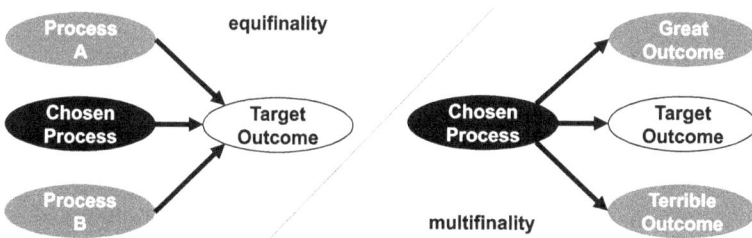

Figure 1.5 Equifinality and multifinality

An example of equifinality is when different product development teams working at different companies with different resources and following different processes could all end up building a nearly identical product (i.e., Target Outcome). We see specific cases of equifinality in common products like cell phones, and payment services apps. Yes, there are differences in feature sets and customer preferences, but a modern cell phone will connect you to another modern cell phone, and the many payment service apps will enable you to send and receive money.

An example of multifinality is when different teams within the same company, presumably following the company formal processes, experience very different results. Team A launches a product that achieves a great outcome, while the product launched by Team B experiences a terrible outcome or outright failure. We see examples of multifinality in the successes and failures within prominent companies such as the successful Macintosh

LC versus the unsuccessful Macintosh Portable or the popular Microsoft Office platform versus the dismal Windows ME operating system.[66]

There are two important takeaways from equifinality and multifinality. First, one process is not *necessarily* any better than another process to achieve a desired goal. Second, a process that seemed to have led to a successful outcome in the past may today lead us where we don't want to go. The historical framework of process development may help explain certain questionable beliefs we have in our business processes. In *Equifinality in Project Management Exploring Causal Complexity in Projects,*[67] the author notes (italics are mine):

- The field of project management has been dominated since 1969 by a prescriptive paradigm that places an emphasis on process control and the *artificial separation of planning from execution.*

- This emphasis stems from an engineering closed-systems tradition, which *assumes that projects can be isolated from their environment, broken down into predictable parts, and manipulated like machines* to achieve the desired results, with certain specifications and under certain controlled initial conditions.

- *Goals are predetermined, objectives are clear, the sequence of activities is prescheduled,* and it is just a matter of the managers, who are accountable for any deviation or change, supervising the execution of plans.

- These techniques are very effective when they are applied to environments with predictable activities with clear goals, controllable sequences, and predictable results like manufacturing, *but in the case of innovation projects, which regularly involve fuzzy missions and goals, with objectives that are not clearly rooted in a fixed reality, and where solutions need time to emerge within complex and emergent social processes, these techniques have been found lacking.*

- Given that the prescriptive paradigm provides universal predefined solutions, there is *the implicit assumption that it can predict project conditions accurately, which leads to overlooking the need to provide methods that allow for flexible management.*

In a similar vein, *Causal Complexity of New Product Development Processes* discusses how the cause and effect of actions and outcomes becomes more difficult to ascertain as the complexity of a project increases (italics is mine):

> The outcomes of new product development (NPD) processes are dependent on the interplay of several interdependent activities. One product development activity can be dependent on the presence or absence of other activities, different kinds of NDP processes may lead to the same outcome, and specific kinds of activities may have a positive effect in one process but no effect in other processes. However, *we currently lack the means to examine and explain this causal complexity inherent in NPD processes.*[68]

Having spent many years in process-driven environments, I have personally promoted various formal business processes, urging my associates that if we remain true to the prescribed procedures and methods, then we *will* achieve success. In these instances when a process is deemed sacrosanct and passionately defended by its faithful practitioners, poor outcomes can easily be blamed on individuals' incompetence rather than a fault in the process. An unfortunate result of solely faulting the practitioners of a process is that dubious processes can be repeatedly used without anyone seriously challenging their reliability to achieve a desired outcome. In the worst case, practitioners may agree that the process they are following isn't working but won't speak up for fear of openly challenging the majority view or attracting the ire of leadership. In such situations, a fatalistic view of the environment may evolve where otherwise engaged and productive professionals resign themselves to just go with the flow and not create any waves.

Equifinality and multifinality inform us that just because we believe that a given formal business process offers a clear path to a certain end doesn't make it so. Of course, this is not to say that all business processes are useless, but our belief in the value of any formal process should be regularly challenged to confirm that it is useful. Our challenges ought to also include so-called *best practices*.

Best Practices

Challenging a person's mental models and favored processes can create a lot of tension and even anger. What can make challenges to our business processes particularly difficult is when we believe a process to be a dependable *best practice*, "a procedure that has been shown by research and experience to produce optimal results and that is established or proposed as a standard suitable for widespread adoption."[69] As I explained earlier, however, equifinality and multifinality ought to remind us to be wary of any claims that even our best practices are suitable for widespread adoption or will achieve desired results.

Many of us who have been tasked to *make things happen* have sought out methods within formal business processes that might help provide a reliable path to success. It's not unusual for employers to require formal training and certification in one or more popular business processes, believing that the investment in time and money will achieve smoother operations and better outcomes. Having been trained in various processes, however, I have often felt that the promised benefits were oversold (unintentionally or deliberately). Further, such training is often unquestionably accepted by companies and their employees as truly *the* best.

For all the time, energy, and money that has been and will be spent on training in best practice business processes, you might wonder why there are still many instances of poor results and outright failures today? What's going on? Are many practitioners lazy, stupid, or just not implementing the processes properly? Are practitioners being forced to veer from the process by higher authorities in the organization to achieve mandated delivery dates?[70] Or, is it possible that business best practices can't be adequately researched and regularly tested and so may be no better than other practices that some may consider subpar?

For example, a former employer created a training manual for planning marketing activities. A compendium of marketing best practices that were designed to create successful programs, the manual was well made with thick paper and color-coded tabs, and oozed confidence. But the stated best practices seemed lacking to me for several reasons, including:

- The manual did not reference any actual successful marketing project that resulted from anyone following the best practices described in the manual.
- There weren't any examples of project successes offered during the live classroom training that accompanied the manual.
- I knew of no other manager who had achieved success by using the stated best practices—not one, although I did ask many other managers about their experiences.

Perhaps there were well-documented successes attributable to the proposed best practices that were never revealed for some reason. It seems to me an odd omission to not share successes, but I also acknowledge that success stories are anecdotal and lack robust metrics and methods to objectively determine the effectiveness of a process or the designation of a best practice.

On another occasion at another firm, I spoke with a senior manager about discrepancies that I saw between business processes that the company claimed to be following and how employees were actually operating daily. I felt that the inconsistency between claimed processes and actual practice could lead to uncertain or poor outcomes because there was no reliable way to monitor and confirm the usefulness of a process that few seemed to be following. The manager nodded in agreement and confided that he wouldn't drive over a bridge that the company built—fortunately, the company wasn't in the business of bridge-building! The manager's metaphorical comment, however, is not unusual and underscores the kind of *Kabuki theater* that I have repeatedly witnessed where claimed adherence to a business process was more style than substance. In the absence of rigorous objective testing and evidence, who's to say if proclaimed best practices are actually being followed or really achieve desired outcomes even if they are being faithfully pursued?

In *Metrics for Measuring Product Development Cycle Time*, researchers examined 35 projects for claims that a quality function deployment process (QFD) decreased both product development cycle time and cost. The researchers reported (italics are the authors'):

> In no instance was *inarguable* evidence that QFD had measurably improved development cycle time or cost uncovered. The primary problem of evaluating QFD's impact at these firms was that no one had ever specifically measured how long product development took prior to implementing QFD. There were no baseline measures from which to form comparisons.[71]

Likewise, the State Education Resource Center of Connecticut (SERC) makes the point that best practices may not reliably lead to desired results (italics are mine):[72]

> The term Best Practice has been used to describe what works in a particular situation or environment. As good consumers of information, *we must keep in mind that a particular practice that has worked for someone within a given set of variables may or may not yield the same results across educational environments.*
>
> Professional wisdom allows educators and family members to adapt to specific circumstances or environments in an area in which research evidence may be absent or incomplete. But *without at least some empirical evidence, education cannot resolve competing approaches, generate cumulative knowledge, and avoid fads and personal biases.*

Ironically, the way that students are trained may make them *less* likely to challenge processes and best practice later in life. In their paper, *On Teaching Critical Thinking to Engineering Students*, the authors observed:

> … engineering and science training can discourage critical thinking by presenting the student with only well-established theories and best practices during the student's training, not requiring a critical attitude from the students. This is indispensable for teaching students the correct methods and techniques but may leave them unprepared to face real life situations, where uncertain, unreliable, or even misleading information can affect the decision process.[73]

Adding another layer of doubt to the moniker of best practices is that situational changes can occur so quickly or so slowly as to hide in plain sight. A consequence of change is that even highly regarded best practices may not work as they once seemed to do. Determining when the limits of a best practice effectiveness are exceeded and are no longer useful can be as difficult as hitting a fastball or detecting the growth of your fingernails over the next minute.

Even if conditions are stable over time, all other things being equal, the effort required to objectively demonstrate that a practice is *the* best by some measure would be practically impossible. Practitioners would need to somehow apply different processes to numerous identical projects under identical conditions (e.g., staff, budget, market) to see if a significant difference in outcomes could be detected. Further, even if companies were able to rewind the clock and re-run a successful project with the same initial conditions but following a different process, what would be their incentive to do so? Why would a company that is achieving acceptable revenues and profits want to tinker with their operations and possibly experience poorer outcomes (even though better outcomes may be achieved by a better, best practice)?

The point is that while formal business processes can be helpful, the designation of *best* is likely more an article of faith than a rigorously demonstrated fact. Consider, too, that adoption of a business process or best practice may represent official, institutionalized groupthink that is resistant to dissenting voices. If an enterprise mandates formal business processes and best practices that the C-Suite believes will lead to better outcomes, then how likely is it that dissenting voices will be raised and heard? Consequently, even best practices should not be shielded from critical challenges by modern Devil's Advocacy. If a modern Devil's Advocate's challenge reveals potential weaknesses that may confound a desired result, then the enterprise may be incentivized to find alternate routes to the desired goal outside of prescribed business processes and best practices via *trailblazing*.

Trailblazing

By *trailblazing*, I mean activities that are not able to be definitely ascertained, calculated, or identified. Unlike activities that can benefit from well-defined and proven trailing processes, trailblazing activities do not have a clear and reliable path to follow. Attempts to use a trailing process for trailblazing activities can lead us headlong into new and unknown obstacles while distracting us from new and more efficient paths to successful outcomes.

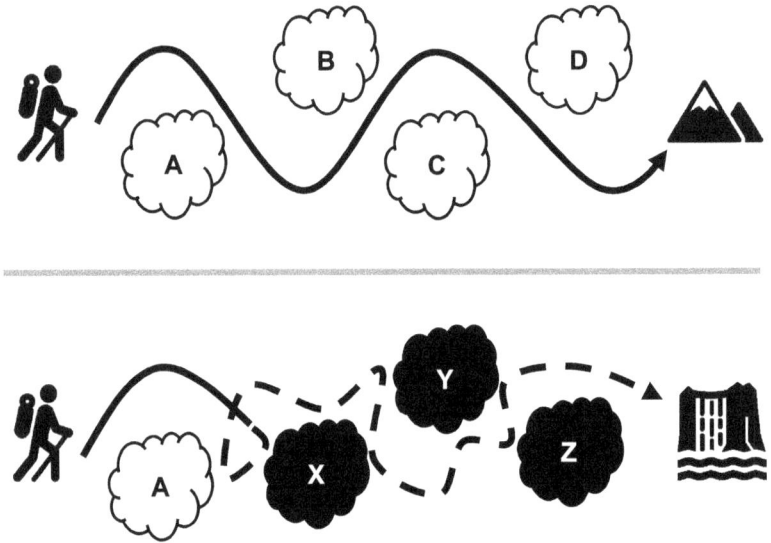

Figure 1.6 A trailing process (top) applied to a trailblazing situation (bottom)

Projects that require trailblazing include innovation creation, the development of truly disruptive products and services, and so on. Unlike trailing business processes that offer reliable paths to follow, trailblazing is more like parachuting into a wilderness and then trying to find your way out.

Consider the article, *What Your Innovation Process Should Look Like*, co-authored by Steve Blank, the well-known entrepreneur who developed the Stanford University course on the lean startup methodology. The article proposes a process for innovation and includes the authors' observations:[74]

- Organizations often pursued innovation without following a disciplined process.

- In the absence of a disciplined process, decisions were often based on presentation skills and politics rather than on any requirement to obtain evidence (e.g., customer interviews and testing of minimally viable products [MVPs]).
- The valuation of proposed innovations is made by committees of "well-intentioned, smart people."

The authors concluded that a need exists for a "self-regulating, evidence-based innovation pipeline." They propose a "canonical Lean Innovation process" that is intended to better curate and prioritize proposed innovations, creating substantial evidence in support of developing an innovation before engineering resources are involved. Note the authors' choice above of the word *canonical*, one definition of which is "a regulation or dogma decreed by a church council"[75] (perhaps the issues facing the modern Devil's Advocate are not so different from those confronting the original Devil's Advocates). The *chapters* of the authors' proposed *canon* are as follows:

- Innovation sourcing to generate a "list of problems, ideas, and technologies that might be worth investing in."
- Curation whereby those tasked with innovation "talk to colleagues and customers" to identify existing common issues, solutions, and the building of an MVP that expresses a possible solution to a problem.
- Prioritization of the proposed innovation for development. Note that at the time of the article, the authors recommended using the McKinsey Three Horizons Model, but a couple of years later, questioned the merits of the model in certain disruptive environments.[76]
- Solution exploration and hypothesis testing that is conducted by the innovation team over a six- to 10-week period. During this time, the team generates a model that defines typical business questions (e.g., the customer need, market, etc.). At this stage, the team may feel that they have a compelling case to move the innovation into an engineering phase or have concluded that the innovation lacks sufficient merit to proceed.

- Incubation during which time "teams championing the projects gather additional data about the application, further build the MVP, and get used to working together."
- Integration and refactoring, which contemplate either assimilation of the innovation development into an existing organization or as a separate division or business entity and stabilizing the MVP while adjusting the team to enable scaling the innovation in production.

You may agree that the proposed innovation process seems reasonable on its face, but I invite you to put on your modern Devil's Advocate's hat and ask yourself some questions about the process. Do the proposed steps define a trailing process in its compartmentalized and stepwise format? Do the proposed steps suggest certitude that the desired outcome *will* be achieved? Has the proposed cannon been robustly *tested and proven* likely to lead to the desired outcome? What role may equifinality and multifinality play in this process? Is the outcome of the process, in other words, as reliable as the map of a well-marked hiking trail?

To be clear, I'm not stating that all business processes are useless, rather that we need to understand and regularly confirm the kind of situation we are facing and determine if a trailing process or trailblazing effort is appropriate. By recognizing the differences between trailing processes and trailblazing situations, we can help establish more reasonable expectations in stakeholders and how we approach uncertainty. The usefulness and selection of trailing business processes and trailblazing activities depend in part on their intertwined, transitional relationship.

Trailing–Trailblazing Transitions

Trailing business processes emerge from trailblazing activities and may revert to trailblazing activities when they are no longer found to be useful or effective. Trailing processes and trailblazing co-exist in two connected hemispheres.

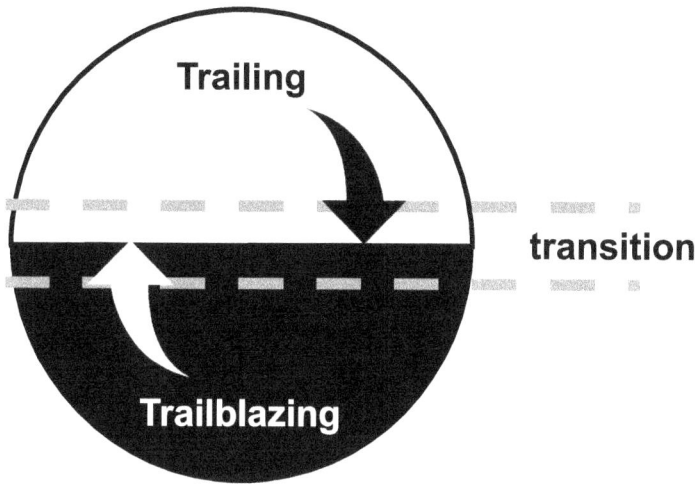

Figure 1.7 The hemispheres of trailing processes and trailblazing activities

The bright trailing hemisphere contains formal processes where relationships are *deterministic*, "phenomena are causally determined by preceding events or natural laws."[77] Of course, business processes don't follow *natural laws* as do the planets and aren't likely proven as are processes like handwashing. Unfortunately, our mental models may mistakenly equate these different kinds of processes. The trailing hemisphere is illuminated by evidence and a history of repeated successes (ideally achieved by many different practitioners). In the dark trailblazing hemisphere, causes and effects are uncertain, and the proof of reliability is lacking. While we are in the trailblazing hemisphere, we can spend a lot of time and effort following paths that lead to dead ends and pushing our way past daunting obstacles. Trailing processes emerge from trial-and-error activities that are conducted in the trailblazing hemisphere and transition into the hemisphere of trailing processes.

Consider a simple example where you attempt to bake pumpernickel bread, a kind of bread you have never made and for which you have no recipe. You may start with a recipe for wheat bread then quickly find yourself trailblazing. Through trial-and-error experimentation, and many failed loaves of bread, you eventually figure out the required list of ingredients, baking temperature, baking time, and so on. If you are successful in making many loaves of quality pumpernickel breads, then your trail-blazing efforts would have led to a new trailing process (i.e., a reliable recipe for pumpernickel bread that others can confidently follow).

There exists a transition threshold between the dark hemisphere of trailblazing and bright hemisphere of trailing processes. That threshold is vague, but hopefully, the transition from trailblazing to a trailing process will occur only if and when success is objectively demonstrated by many practitioners over many instances of its use.[78] As was discussed earlier under *Best Practices* and *Equifinality and Multifinality*, the ability to obtain objective and sufficient evidence for the reliability and usefulness of formal business processes is practically impossible. Further, trailing processes may fall back into the trailblazing hemisphere when they are no longer useful in achieving desired goals. When trailing business processes stumble, then they may undergo modification to regain their usefulness or may be abandoned altogether. Transition examples include the shift within firms from older project management processes like waterfall to newer lean thinking and agile methods (which some argue have become less useful than initially hoped for).[79]

Trailblazing activities may begin on a trailing process path; however, we need to recognize that a trailing process we select may not be the path we ought to stay on for the duration of our journey. Recall the warning above that a *prescriptive paradigm* includes "the implicit assumption that it can predict project conditions accurately, which leads to overlooking the need to provide methods that allow for flexible management."[80] Failing to acknowledge the limited predictive power of formal business processes and stubbornly following a map of dubious usefulness may lead us deeper into the woods rather than to our desired destination.

If you agree that we regularly and confidently apply business processes and best practices without much thought, then you may also wonder why this behavior is so? We touched on some of the possible factors, including managers making an honest but mistaken process selection and cases when a process is intentionally misused to shift responsibility. Perhaps, the strongest force on our preference for trailing processes is our human desire for simple answers and absolute certainty.

In their book, *Superforecasting: The Art and Science of Prediction*, the authors note the differences between those who tend to rely upon a narrow view and speak with confidence about future outcomes (the authors refer to these people as *hedgehogs*) and those who take a more diverse view that considers a range of likely future outcomes (the authors refer to these people as *foxes*). The authors found that the foxes do a better job forecasting than do the hedgehogs. However, even when popular hedgehog forecasters like those featured on television news and talk shows get it very wrong, they are still sought out for their opinion! Why? The authors' explanation for hedgehog forecaster fame is that "The simplicity and confidence of the hedgehog impairs foresight, but it calms nerves—which is good for the careers of hedgehogs."[81]

Our desire for calm nerves notwithstanding, our human nature seems to cloud our ability to consider many of the issues raised earlier. Behavioral scientists tell us that we normally operate on autopilot without much rational, analytical processing. As we'll see below, our biases and fallacious reasoning may reinforce our faith in business processes to the detriment of our judgments and outcomes.

Bias and Fallacy

The term *cognitive bias* was coined in the 1970s by researchers Amos Tversky and Daniel Kahneman.[82] The term refers to the way that we understand the world, creating our own subjective perception of reality. Researchers point to many, many cognitive biases that likely affect every decision that we make even though we are unaware of our biases.

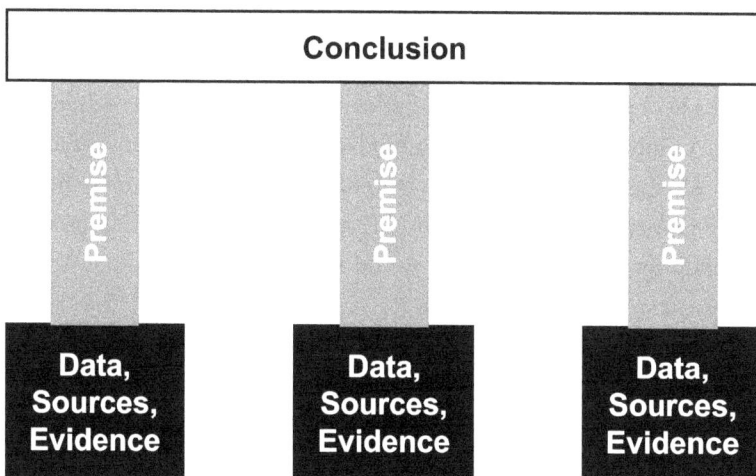

Figure 1.8 Real argument diagram

The term *fallacy* refers to an error in a logical argument or reasoning. By argument, I don't mean a shouting match of the type that regularly plays out political debate, rather a series of statements (premises), based on evidence that support a singular conclusion.

You may conclude that a new product will achieve a certain level of annual revenues based on several premises. Your premises may include that the new product will better meet customer needs, that customers will pay a premium price for a product that better meets their needs, and that your new product will lead to an increase of your market share. Your premises may be based on historical data, market research, input from the sales team, and so forth. Included in the information at your disposal are facts, assumptions, opinions, and beliefs. Factual weaknesses of a premise would weaken the support for the conclusion, but a conclusion may still be useful even without all of the original premises.

There are so many biases and fallacies that may weaken our judgments that it would be impractical to memorize all of them. However, it may be useful for the modern Devil's Advocate to always look for at least 10 that follow, which I feel are common and especially effective in interfering with quality decision making.

Ad Hominem Fallacy

The Latin term *ad hominem* means "to the person." This term may have originally been intended as an acceptable rhetorical method to sway the opinion of an audience but has come to be held in contempt. A common example of the ad hominem fallacy is when in a political debate one party attacks her opponent rather than her opponent's argument. For example, Party A proposes a tax increase to fund an initiative, and Party B accuses Party A of being a socialist rather than offering any rebuttal to the merits of the proposed tax increase. Even if Party A willingly acknowledges that she endorses socialism, that fact would not mean that the proposed tax increase is meritless.

Note that not all ad hominem arguments are unrelated to reasoned decision making. The reputation of the little boy who repeatedly and falsely cried wolf may be something to consider the next time he raises the alarm. However, it is possible that his next wolf alert is truthful, so a challenge analysis should be made on the boy's claim and not solely his character. The ad hominem ought to always catch the attention of a modern Devil's Advocate.

False Dilemma Fallacy

A *dilemma* is a choice between two options. Also referred to as *either-or* and *all or nothing*, this fallacy is often presented as a false dichotomy when just two completely opposed choices are identified or offered. It is certainly true that either-or decisions are made all the time (e.g., turn left or turn right); however, in many instances, black and white options are intentionally or naïvely offered and thereby limit useful alternatives. For example, a business may consider only continuing to sell an old product that generates low profit margins or to discontinue the product. Other options may include updating or bundling the product to improve the value proposition and profitability or licensing the product to another company that sells into non-competitive markets. Either-or judgments can be a very effective red flag alert to the Devil's Advocate for further exploration into alternate options that weren't identified or pursued.

Survivorship Bias

Survivorship bias causes us to consider only successful outcomes (i.e., *survivors*). This bias can lead us to conclude clear cause-and-effects where none may actually exist. By focusing solely on survivors, we remain oblivious to many other potential failures. For example, it's not uncommon to see mostly positive success stories on social media. Simple narratives are generated about how successful celebrities and businesses achieved their success and readers are encouraged that they, too, can be successful if they just follow the advice provided in the simple narrative. A closer examination, however, reveals that success is hardly guaranteed by any simple formula, and that about half of new businesses in the United States fail within five years' time.[83] Judgments that are set upon rosy and anecdotal success stories that ignore lesser-known failures ought to be of high interest to the modern Devil's Advocate.

Confirmation Bias

Confirmation bias occurs when we readily accept information that conforms to an established belief that we hold dear and readily reject information that challenges the belief. If, for example, you believe that a certain economic policy will lead to positive results, then you are likely to point to any information that supports that view and discount information that refutes that view. Your belief may be so strong that you simply cannot accept strong contradictory evidence. Confirmation bias may unconsciously simplify our mental models of the world, so we don't have to constantly challenge a perspective or course of action. Confirmation bias may also help reduce *cognitive dissonance,* the discomfort we experience when trying to hold two contradictory ideas in our mind. Although some beliefs may be based on strong objective evidence, belief-based mental models, processes, and best practices are rich targets for challenge analysis by the modern Devil's Advocate.

False Cause Fallacy

False cause fallacy is exhibited when a series of events are incorrectly taken to indicate a cause-and-effect relationship. This fallacy can occur when correlation is confused with causation. *Correlation* can be viewed as relationships between two or more items that aren't likely due to chance alone but may not be causal. *Causation* is when one thing leads to another.

The rise in homicides relative to ice cream sales, shown in the following first diagram, does not likely prove that an increase in ice cream sales causes an increase in homicides. It is more likely that the seasonal temperature causes both ice cream sales and homicides to increase as shown in the second diagram. A business example may be a decision to purchase more advertising that seemed to drive sales in the past without regard for factors other than the advertising promotion such as seasonality, price reductions, or a switch due to a competitor's temporary backlog. The practice of modern Devil's Advocacy may include challenging claimed cause-and-effect relationships in a decision.

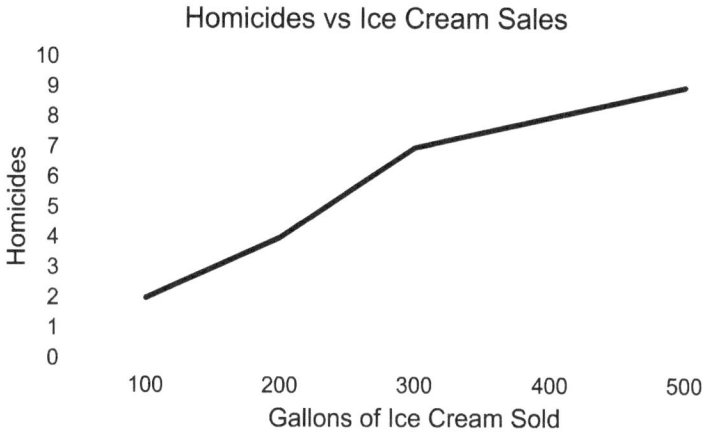

Figure 1.9 Correlation example

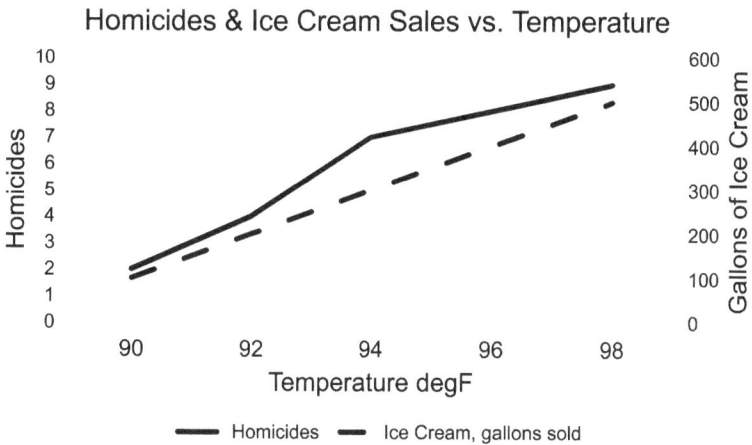

Figure 1.10 Causation example

Fundamental Attribution Bias

Also known as fundamental attribution error, this bias occurs when we attribute a person's behavior to their personality rather than to external factors. Claiming that a person is completely responsible for a crime suffered by them (i.e., *victim blaming*) is an example of this bias. Another example is making a judgment about a person based solely on what you observe rather than considering the reason for the person's behavior—an abrupt stop of a car in front of yours may be due to the driver avoiding a collision rather than just poor driving skill.

Reflect on your own experience where you may have felt that someone was acting unreasonably until you learned that they were saddled with an impossible workload and dealing with difficult family issues. During a challenge analysis, the Devil's Advocate may encounter claims made by decision makers that were misinterpretations of actions taken by others.

Halo Effect Bias

Halo effect bias is the tendency for an impression created in one area to influence opinion in another area. This effect was popularized by Phil Rosenzweig in his seminal book, *The Halo Effect,*[84] in which he describes the halo phenomenon in the business world as, "The tendency to look at a company's overall performance and make attributions about its culture, leadership, values, and more. In fact, many things we commonly claim drive company performance are simple attributions based on prior performance." This bias has an earlier reference in a 1915 study, *A Constant Error in Psychological Ratings.*[85]

Authors of the 1915 study observed how individual employees and officers seemed to receive high marks in several different attributes that might not be necessarily connected (e.g., intelligence, industry, technical skill, reliability). It was as if the persons grading the individuals saw one outstanding attribute and then placed a *halo* upon the individual for all attributes without close examination of evidence that would support each individual attribute.

The modern Devil's Advocate will want to consider such halos around individuals, teams, and companies, especially when these entities are claimed to be extraordinary performers. These claims may be true to some measure, but as investment firms remind us, past performance is no guarantee of future results. When a potential halo is identified, the Devil's Advocate will want to probe further into how that perception of an individual, team, or company may have affected the judgment that she is challenging.

Framing Bias

Framing bias refers to the tendency for our perceptions and decisions to be influenced by how information is presented to promote an agenda or ideology. In the left column of the following table is an actual e-mail that I received from a local politician with the subject line, "I Need Your Feedback; Do You Support Earmarks?" In the right column is a version that I modified (italics are mine):

Table 1.1 Framing bias example

Original e-mail	Modified e-mail
Recently, some members of Congress have expressed wanting to revive earmarks—a legislative procedure that allows for spending carve-outs for specific projects *historically fraught with waste*. Do you support or oppose lifting the ban on earmarks?	Recently, some members of Congress have expressed wanting to revive earmarks—a legislative procedure that allows for spending carve-outs for specific projects that *will bring much-needed jobs to our State*. Do you support or oppose lifting the ban on earmarks?

Reading the original e-mail on the left, you may feel as though earmarks should be avoided because you don't want your tax dollars wasted, especially when this waste has a long and well-established history. However, the slightly modified message on the right may have you thinking that jobs are good, and with earmarks, come jobs, so maybe you ought to support earmarks? This kind of framing is not only common in the business setting but often encouraged in order to place a judgment in the most positive light. The modern Devil's Advocate should always identify each and every claim and then attempt to see how different frames of the claims could alter a judgment or question the underlying support for a judgment.

Appeal to Authority Fallacy

Appeal to authority fallacy refers to our tendency to accept that a claim is true because *an authority* made the claim. Note that the term authority can apply either to someone who has the power to mandate a decision or to an expert who has a high level of knowledge and experience in certain subject matter. These are two very different kinds of authorities.

An example of the first kind of authority may be the CEO of a company or government official who can impose a decision regardless of her area of expertise. An example of the second kind of authority may be a researcher who holds advanced degrees in a certain area of knowledge, who has published numerous peer-reviewed articles, and who others in the field acknowledge as a thought leader. Claims made by either kind of authority may be false or weak; however, it is reasonable to seek out the perspective of those authorities who have appropriate subject knowledge and expertise.

It is also beneficial, of course, to consider the view of several with subject matter expertise, when possible, rather than to be led solely by a singular authority's opinion. Steve Ballmer, former CEO of Microsoft, famously opined on the iPhone announcement that it was too expensive and would not "appeal to business customers because it doesn't have a keyboard."[86] Warren Buffet, one of the most successful investors in the world, answered when asked why he didn't make an early investment in Amazon that "I didn't understand the power of the model as I went along. And the price always seemed to more than reflect the power of the model at that time."[87]

Dunning–Kruger Effect Bias

Coined in 1999 by Cornell University psychologists David Dunning and Justin Kruger, the Dunning–Kruger effect is a bias where we are unable to recognize our own incompetence. Not only do we not recognize our incompetence, but we also may grossly underestimate the depth of our ineptitude. Dunning and Kruger arrived at their conclusion as reported in their article, *Unskilled and Unaware of It*,[88] which examined individuals' self-assessments of performance against their actual scores.

The first thing you'll notice in the diagram is that the perceived scores are higher than the actual scores in the first three groups. Those with the lowest actual scores also estimated their performance much more poorly than those with higher actual scores. A curious thing happens in the top 25 percent where individuals with the highest actual scores believed that they performed worse than they had. In case you feel as

Actual vs Perceived Score

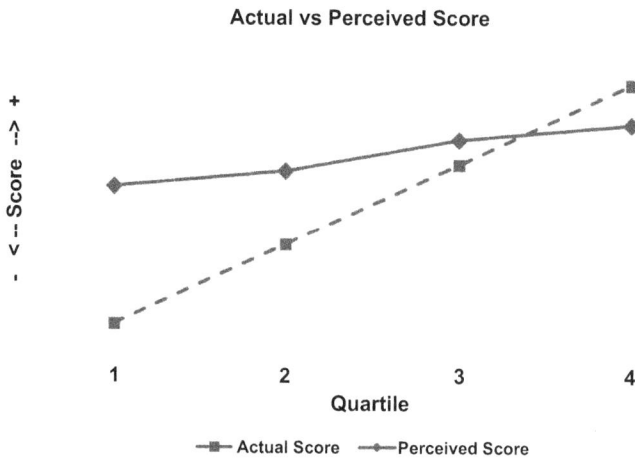

Figure 1.11 *Dunning–Kruger effect bias*

though you are better at estimating your abilities than the Dunning–Kruger test subjects, I refer you to a caution by Dr. Dunning, "The first rule of the Dunning-Kruger club is you don't know you're a member of the Dunning-Kruger club."[89] Dunning is a proponent of modern Devil's Advocacy as a means to counter the Dunning–Kruger effect and advises, "For individuals, the trick is to be your own devil's advocate: to think through how your favored conclusions might be misguided; to ask yourself how you might be wrong, or how things might turn out differently from what you expect."[90]

Remember that the biases and fallacies noted earlier are just a few of the many that regularly cloud our judgments. These are human failings that we all share but rarely think about or recognize their influence on our decision making. Because we interact with others on a regular basis, including for judgments that are made in group settings, the interactions of each individual's biases and fallacious reasoning can create complex environments that are challenging to understand and navigate. Under certain circumstances, diversity of thought and perspective offered by a group can be powerful. Contrary to the popular belief, however, crowds don't always improve decision making and outcomes.

Crowds Are Not Necessarily Wise

You may be familiar with the claim that estimates made by a large group of people offer results that are more accurate than those of experts? Does this claim lead you to believe that a majority decision will be a wise decision?

Made popular by the book *The Wisdom of Crowds*,[91] this claim traces back to an article by statistician Francis Galton in the March 1907 publication of *Nature*. Galton's article was entitled *Vox Populi*, which is Latin for the *voice of the people* and a term that is commonly used to mean a majority opinion. In his article, Galton describes a weight-judging competition held at an annual stock and poultry exhibition. Participants secretly marked on ballots their guess for the actual *dressed weight* of a (presumably) live ox, which is the weight after the "hide, head, feet, and gut are removed."[92] Galton noted:

> The competitors included butchers and farmers, some of whom were highly expert in judging the weight of cattle; others were probably guided by such information as they might pick up, and by their own fancies. The average competitor was probably as well fitted for making a just estimate of the dressed weight of the ox, as an average voter is of judging the merits of most political issues on which he votes, and the variety among the voters to judge justly was probably much the same in either case.[93]

If Galton's subjective estimate of the crowd composition was correct, then you might reasonably expect that the weight estimates for the ox were not particularly influenced by expertise. After all, the crowd was not made up solely of butchers, farmers, and others with experience and skill in estimating the weight of livestock.[94] So, how well did this average crowd of people do in estimating the dressed weight of the ox?

After plotting out the weight guesses from 787 ballots, Galton determined that the "middlemost estimate" (i.e., the median) was 1,207 pounds versus the actual weight of the ox at 1,198 pounds (a bit high by 9 lb., or 0.8 percent the actual weight). Galton stated that the result was "more creditable to the trustworthiness of a democratic judgment than might have been expected."

As with many popular stories, certain claims based on the Galton article are stated as fact, although the truth is more nuanced. For example, some have suggested that "Galton found evidence that the median estimate of a group can be more accurate than estimates of experts."[95] In fact, Galton did not compare a subset of livestock expert estimates against the estimates of the other participants, did not report if the winners of the competition were experts, and did not make the specific assertion that any group estimate can beat any expert estimate.

Galton's very brief article has been revisited by researchers who do support the idea that some group estimations can result in remarkably accurate results. There appears, however, to be a set of four required conditions to achieve accurate crowd estimates:

1. Diversity of expertise (not everyone in the group is a butcher, physician, psychiatrist, etc.)
2. Diversity of opinion (not everyone holds the same perspective)
3. Estimates are not influenced by the group (individual estimates are not shared with other group members)
4. Information is aggregated (all of the estimates are collected and examined in a *centralized* way)

Ensuring that the preceding conditions are met is quite a challenge, especially in the typical business team setting. For one thing, teams generally do not include hundreds of members who opine on a singular metric like the dressed weight of an ox. Members of relatively small project teams have likely worked together before, hold some commonly held assumptions and beliefs about the project, and share their opinions. As science writer Philip Ball observed, such conditions may lead to unwise group decisions (italics are mine):

> ... researchers found that, as the amount of information participants were given about each other's guesses increased, the range of their guesses got narrower, and the centre of this range could drift further from the true value. In other words, the groups were tending towards a consensus, to the detriment of accuracy. *This finding challenges a common view in management and politics that it is best to seek consensus in group decision making.* What you can end up with instead is herding towards a relatively arbitrary position.[96]

You may also wonder about the presumed wisdom of crowds the further one travels from simple black-and-white issues for which there may be a clearly defined and objectively verifiable metric. In his review of *The Wisdom of Crowds*, psychology researcher Dr. Geoffrey Sutton asked (italics are mine):

> … can we trust the crowd to make wise decisions in moral matters? Are the historical examples of crowds choosing to follow leaders in destructive acts representative of the impaired wisdom of crowds? We may also ask if indeed the four conditions are necessary for crowds to make wise decisions, then *why are crowds not wise enough to create such conditions?*[97]

These same kinds of questions would certainly apply to the real-world issues that business teams face when estimating beyond relatively simple questions like market size and price sensitivity (e.g., what should Facebook and Twitter do about the misinformation that is circulated via their platforms). Here, too, I propose that modern Devil's Advocacy can offer useful challenges to encourage more thoughtful consideration of important, complex issues.

Any method of decision making has its strengths and weaknesses, and various decision-making methodologies may be employed depending on factors like the group composition and the environment in which the group operates. When interacting with multicultural teams, unexpressed but impactful miscommunication issues within the stakeholder entity may be common and confound the modern Devil's Advocate's efforts.[98] Although it may be a natural desire of group members to go along together and reach harmonious decisions, groups may benefit by enabling (if not outright encouraging) thoughtful dissent. As the late Supreme Court Justice Antonin Scalia acknowledged, "I probably believe that the worst opinions in my court have been unanimous. Because there's nobody on the other side pointing out all the flaws."[99]

Modern Devil's Advocates will rarely challenge decisions made by one person but rather will examine how a group of individuals has made judgments and reached conclusions. Of particular interest to the modern Devil's Advocate will be signs of rote decision making that may indicate groupthink, which can be reinforced by dogmatic processes and best practices. Understanding the dynamics of dissent within organizations can help modern Devil's Advocates remain alert for signs of useful dissent that can be leveraged in their challenge analyses.

Organizational Dissent and Group Decisions

The level of support for a decision may be determined by the expressed and implied dissent within a group, and decisions that are imposed on others can increase the chance of dissent. Although those who mandate a decision may be unwilling or unable to hear opposing voices, openness to honest dissent can be beneficial to decision makers and stakeholders alike, depending on how the dissent is addressed. Research on organizational dissent dynamics[100] has identified three forms of dissent in an enterprise: upward, latent, and displaced.

- **Upward dissent** is when an employee provides open dissent to a higher level with the goal of making an improvement. The dissenter expects that their honest dissent will be heard and acknowledged. If ignored or not followed up, then upward dissenters can shift their position to either a latent or displaced dissenter.
- **Latent dissent** is described as antagonistic—the kind of dissent that is shared with other employees but not offered to a higher level. Latent dissenters don't expect any response from a higher level and may fear retribution if they openly express their views. Because higher levels aren't aware of latent dissent, they may operate under the false impression that *everyone is onboard* with a decision.
- **Displaced dissent** is when dissenters expect retaliation from management for expressions of dissent. This kind of dissent may lead to the dissenter involving third parties outside of their organization such as to journalists or regulatory agencies.

Upward dissent may lead to a kind of fatigue within the upper management of an entity and to a lower tolerance by upper management for open dissent. The research suggests that "… perceived management responsiveness to dissent will be impacted negatively when major decisions concerning the members, or the direction of the institution are made without their consultation or when their concerns are not timely and respectfully addressed. Accordingly, some employees will disengage and join the [latent dissenters]." Shifting dissent type from open and upward to either latent or displaced may create significant problems within an organization in a relatively short period of time.

The tone and focus of a group that is composed of compatible personas with similar skills will likely be very different from the tone and focus of a more diverse group. Getting a sense of the stakeholders who participated in a decision may be helpful in revealing dynamics that intentionally or naïvely biased the judgment. The modern Devil's Advocate typically won't have the time or the need to conduct a formal evaluation of personalities such as the Myers and Briggs[101] personality assessment. Rather, the modern Devil's Advocate can seek a quick estimate of the push and pull that might exist among the decision-making stakeholders. Authors of the article *Great Teams Are About Personalities, Not Just Skills*[102] offered a model of group dynamics that considers stakeholders in both their functional role (title, technical skill) and their psychological role, which includes:

(a) **Results-oriented**. Team members who naturally organize work and take charge tend to be socially self-confident, competitive, and energetic.

(b) **Relationship-focused**. Team members who naturally focus on relationships, are attuned to others' feelings, and are good at building cohesion tend to be warm, diplomatic, and approachable.

(c) **Process and rule followers**. Team members who pay attention to details, processes, and rules tend to be reliable, organized, and conscientious.

(d) **Innovative and disruptive thinkers**. Team members who naturally focus on innovation, anticipate problems, and recognize when the team needs to change tend to be imaginative, curious, and open to new experiences.

(e) **Pragmatic**. Team members who are practical, hard-headed challengers of ideas and theories tend to be prudent, emotionally stable, and level-headed.

As you might have expected, the authors of the article noted that effective teams need to have a balance of personality types. Teams heavy with results-oriented, pragmatic and process-driven stakeholders likely lack sufficient relationship building skills. Likewise, teams light with results-oriented and pragmatic stakeholders may have achieved harmony but at the cost of reliable forward motion. This balancing act of personalities, especially in teams with diverse traits, can lead to strong disagreement and different types of dissent. Opening the door to dissenting voices can be challenging but may also lead to more thoughtful judgments and better outcomes in an enterprise.

It's important to remember that the modern Devil's Advocate is *not* the decision maker for any group but rather acts like a lawyer who builds and presents a compelling case. A widely held decision that the modern Devil's Advocate will find herself challenging will have been formed through one of three different decision-making methods: mandated, unanimous consensus, and consent. Each type of decision making has its own strengths and weaknesses and knowing, which was used may offer useful insight for the modern Devil's Advocate.

Mandated Decisions

Mandated decisions are those that are made by one person (or a small group of people) and then imposed on others who have not participated in the decision-making process. A typical example is when the commander of a military force or the CEO of a business mandates a decision. This decision is then conveyed downward through levels of management to those who will be tasked to achieve a successful outcome.

If you are the CEO at the top of a hierarchy, then you may welcome the autonomous authority of mandates, believing that nothing would happen if you didn't explicitly tell others what to do. Even if you aren't a micromanager, you may believe that leadership demands regular expressions of your executive power, including your authority over the enterprise. Although you can make decisions more quickly if you make decisions by yourself or with a small circle of others in your staff, there are potentially damaging downsides to such high-level, authoritarian control.

As the CEO of a company, you may have little to no understanding about how to design, build, or sell your company's products and services,

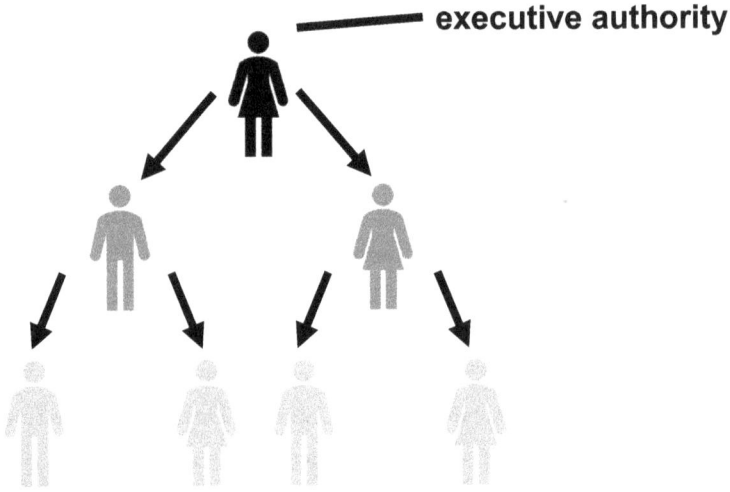

executive authority

Figure 1.12 Mandated decision-making

even if you had such understanding and skill earlier in your career. Limiting decisions to just yourself and close advisors does not likely benefit from a diversity of opinion, information, and expertise. A common analogy for the benefit of diversity is seeking the highest mountain peak where the peak represents an optimal decision.

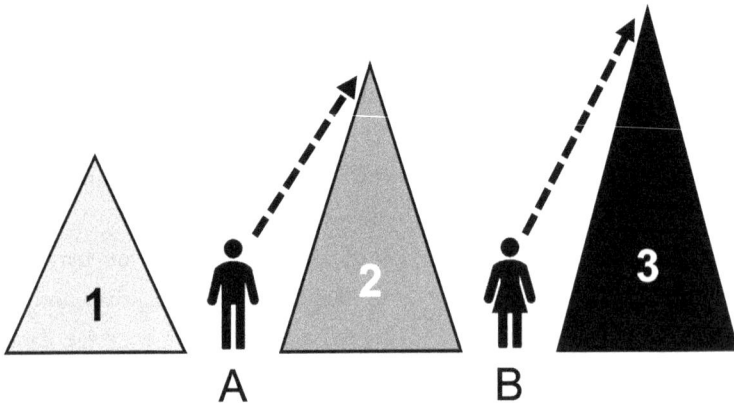

Figure 1.13 Optimum solution search

In the mountain peak analogy, one person (A) spies a mountain peak in his vicinity (2) that he deems is highest (i.e., the best available decision option). Had this person asked others who operate beyond his locality and expertise (B), then he may have learned about an even higher peak or better option (3). Perhaps, intending to drive activities faster, party A may forgo seeking wider input and mandate actions based on his limited perspective. His mandated decision is not optimal, and it will likely impact many elements from design, through customer satisfaction to revenues, and profits.

Mandated decisions can also create an acrimonious environment as employees throughout the firm try to figure out how best to implement a decision in which they were not involved, don't understand, and don't support. Depending on your temperament as the CEO, employees may publicly support you while quietly agreeing among themselves that you are misguided, and your goal is unachievable. Further, it may take months of implementation effort until the full shortcomings of a mandated decision surface, during which time other related decisions have been made, each contributing to an undesirable outcome. An extreme case of how badly mandated decision making can go is Theranos, the company I mentioned earlier where the CEO reportedly had a direct hand in all decisions that led to the firms collapse.

At the same time, mandated decisions may be required, depending on the environment, personnel, time constraints, and other factors. Warfighting is an extreme example where the implications of an overarching mission are so broad that those at the extremities must comply even though they may not fully understand their assigned tasks. Although most CEOs may never face the same kinds of life-and-death decisions that commanders of military operations do, they will certainly be confronted by thorny problems that need to be quickly addressed by a mandated decision. Such instances may include product failures that cause injury or death, sudden disruptions in supply chains that halt the production of products and revenue generation, or unforeseen competitive challenges that diminish the importance of products and services in the development pipeline.

When the modern Devil's Advocate is asked to challenge a decision that was mandated at the executive level, she may very well need to directly question the judgment of the CEO or a vice president. Although such challenges may be tightly tangled with politics and power, the modern Devil's Advocate ought to approach the task with the same prosecutorial vigor as any other challenge analysis. Modern Devil's Advocacy is never about attacking the parties involved in the original decision but in analyzing the evidence and reasoning used to arrive at the original judgment.

It is only through an authentic effort that the modern Devil's Advocate serves her client and the client's stakeholders.

Unanimous Consensus Decisions

Consensus decisions seek unanimity or harmony. The general idea is that a proposed decision is opened to discussion and when everyone agrees then the decision is accepted. We've all had common experiences in consensus decision making outside of the business world, like when choosing a restaurant for a group of friends or family.

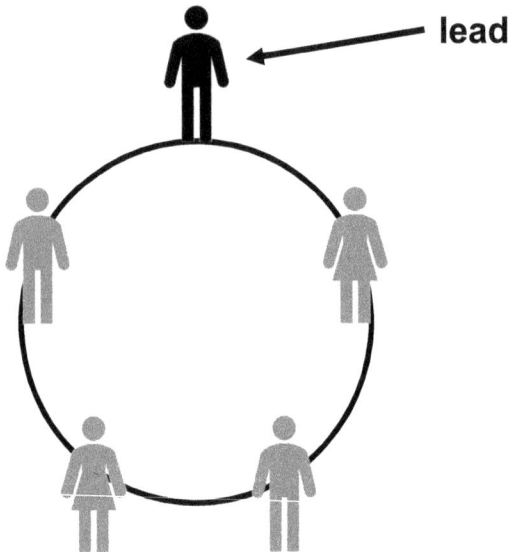

Figure 1.14 Unanimous consensus decision making

If you (the figure at the top of the preceding circle) are tasked to choose a restaurant that will appeal to your team, then attaining unanimous consensus may be quick and easy. Knowing everyone well, you would not propose restaurants that are likely to fail (e.g., no Moroccan, which Frank dislikes, or Italian, which Mary dislikes). Taking this approach, you may always go to one of a handful of restaurants because experience indicates that those restaurants are where everyone seems happiest (even if the menu options have grown stale). This rote behavior is a *red flag* in modern

Devil's Advocacy because it suggests *groupthink* and an imposed limitation of alternate options. The unanimous consensus process can also be long and contentious.

For example, perhaps you are the manager of a team that is tasked to decide which of two proposed product innovations should be pursued. The innovations differ in their reward/risk profile, where the first innovation is relatively simple to accomplish with a small but acceptable return, while the second innovation would be a significant challenge but could offer a much higher reward. In these kinds of cases, the team composition and environment can make consensus very difficult.

Those who will be responsible for the development of the innovation may want to create something new but feel overwhelmed due to the high level of support they currently provide for existing products. This group may be very reluctant to take on any new development work and grudgingly opt for the simpler innovation option. Meanwhile, those responsible for sales may be desperate for new products to sell and so enthusiastically support the more difficult innovation option. Other team members like marketing and operations may be more neutral in their views and could support either option.

Round after round of discussions may lead developers and sales associates to harden their positions. Meanwhile, marketing and operations associates may be swayed to one side or the other due to personal relationships and preferences (e.g., marketing's empathy for sales' perspective and operations affinity for the developers' perspective).

As the team manager, you likely have the responsibility to mediate discussions and help achieve a unanimous consensus. You likely also have the authority to force a mandated decision if the team can't reach unanimous consensus in which case, the same benefits and shortcomings of a mandated decision, as discussed earlier, apply.

Consent Decisions

An alternative to both mandated and unanimous consensus decision making is the *consent* method.[103] Consent decision making is a key element in *Sociocracy*, which in the United States is (unfortunately) confused with *Socialism*, and so often referred to as *Dynamic Governance*.[104,105,106]

The consent decision-making approach is *not* seeking unanimous agreement among all parties in the group, rather, the consent method requires that parties give their assent or approval. The general idea in consent decision making is that everyone participates in creating a decision that everyone will support, even if everyone doesn't agree that the decision is the best decision.

On the surface, consent decision making may seem like an insignificant difference compared to a unanimous consensus, but I've found that consent decision making can be a refreshingly effective approach because it permits strong dissenting views to be expressed while maintaining forward motion on decisions.

There are three main roles in the consent decision-making method: sponsor, facilitator, and stakeholder.

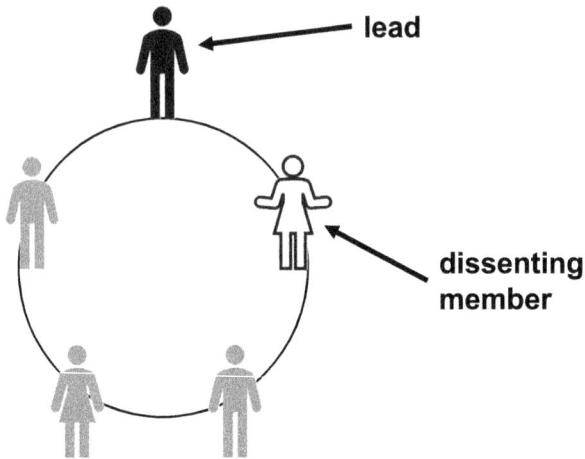

Figure 1.15 Consent decision making

- **Sponsor**. The sponsor is the person who is proposing a decision to the group. The sponsor prepares the proposal after fully researching the question and related issues, speaking with associates offline, and with consideration of the larger goals and constraints of the entity and its stakeholders. The sponsor can hold any title within any department of the organization.

- **Facilitator**. The facilitator is the person who is responsible for the consent method being followed. The facilitator takes notes but doesn't "take sides." In addition to ensuring that everyone is heard during the review of a proposed decision, the facilitator is also tasked to ensure that all paramount objections are addressed. A paramount objection is not a strong opinion or an attempt of a member with authority to lord it over the group. Rather, a paramount objection is some reason the proposed decision would either work against the aims of the group or would somehow prevent the objecting party from supporting the decision.
- **Stakeholder**. Stakeholders include everyone participating in the decision in addition to the sponsor and facilitator. In a typical project team, these members would include representatives from engineering, marketing, sales, operations, legal, finance, and so on.

For example, a decision needs to be made on the feature set of a new product. Marketing and sales have their views based on competitive products and where they believe the market is heading. Engineering and operations have their views based on preferred technologies, current capabilities, and target cost of goods. Legal, finance, and others also have their perspectives, based on their roles and responsibilities.

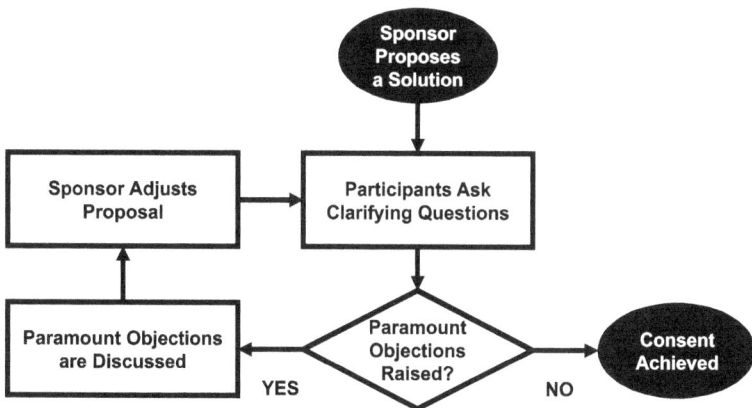

Figure 1.16 Simple consent decision flowchart

A marketing manager is tasked as the sponsor to propose the final feature set and a group of stakeholders is tasked to reach a consent decision. The marketing manager presents the proposed feature set and provides the rationale behind a decision to go with the proposed features. The facilitator, who could be selected from any department, ensures that everyone, in turn, gets the opportunity to ask the sponsor clarifying questions about the proposal. This round is solely intended to ensure that the proposal is fully understood by everyone, neither objections nor counter-arguments are offered, and no decision is sought.

After everyone's clarifying questions are addressed by the sponsor, the facilitator asks individuals of the group in turn if they have any *paramount objections* to the proposal, not if they agree. Paramount objections are *not the opinions* of the stakeholders but the reasons why the proposal could realistically interfere with the stakeholders' ability to support the proposal.

For example, a stakeholder who represents the legal department might object to one of the proposed features because it would infringe on a competitor's patent. A stakeholder who represents the sales department may have a strong opinion about a legal issue; however, her role is not in a legal capacity, and she likely lacks the legal knowledge of her associate from the legal department. In such a case of differing viewpoints, the sales representative could consent while still voicing her opinion.

Paramount objections are addressed by a revision to the proposed decision. In the preceding example, the potential patent-infringing feature may be dropped from the proposal provided it does not raise another paramount objection. Marketing, for example, may raise a paramount objection to dropping a feature because doing so would weaken the final product and cause reduced revenues and profits that no longer meet the requirements of the company. The paramount objection could also be addressed outside of the meeting; for example, legal may agree to take a closer look at potential infringement, and if they find a way to avoid a violation, then would consent to the decision. Through series of rounds, the paramount objections are addressed, the proposal is modified, and a consent decision is made when no further paramount objections are raised.

Note, again, that a consent decision is *not* one of universal agreement, and some stakeholders may have decided differently if the decision was theirs alone. Consent decisions permit everyone to be heard and help to ensure that no one will stand in the way of the decision, which meets the aims of the company. Consent decision making may also help maintain an awareness of uncertainty in assumptions and beliefs, and to promote a willingness by the stakeholders to reexamine decisions as new information and insights are obtained.

While the preceding example led to a successful consent decision, we recognize that in the real world, our human nature will likely cloud our thinking and actions, especially when highly emotional conditions exist. If a stakeholder simply refuses to participate in the consent decision-making method, or if an executive with the authority overrides a consent decision, then participants may find themselves unwilling and unhappy actors in either the unanimous consensus or mandated methods discussed earlier.

Modern Devil's Advocacy Is Useful

As you reflect on the material presented up to this point, you may still be questioning the usefulness of modern Devil's Advocacy. Is it something that could benefit your own decision making and the decision making that your business associates perform daily?

Devil's Advocacy has certainly had its critics from its early inception to today. Undoubtedly, Devil's Advocacy has not always achieved its intended goals over its centuries of use by the Catholic Church. Likewise, the secular community has also questioned the effectiveness of modern Devil's Advocacy. Of the various criticisms raised against Devil's Advocacy today, perhaps the most common one is that it is a form of *inauthentic* dissent that can be more harmful than useful.

Heuer and Pherson note, "If group members see the Devil's Advocacy as an analytic exercise, they have to put up with … this exercise may actually enhance the majority's original belief."[107] Likewise, psychologist Dr. Charlan Nemeth, who has researched and written about the value of dissent, has warned, "Role-playing may actually thwart serious consideration of new alternatives. Armed with the possibly incorrect belief that other options have been considered, thoughts may corroborate one's initial belief and confidence may be inflated."[108,109]

Psychology defines *authenticity* as, "… the extent to which people act coherently with themselves,"[110] but how can we know whether or not dissent is authentic? I don't know of any instrument that reliably and objectively reveals authentic dissent like a digital thermometer reveals body temperature—although that would be a really useful gadget!

Such criticism of inauthenticity is reinforced when modern Devil's Advocacy is framed as a form of *role-playing*. Of course, declaring that *playing* Devil's Advocate is inauthentic dissent is a bit like saying that *playing* doctor is inauthentic medicine. Someone simply going through the motions of modern Devil's Advocacy without investing any effort in thinking and analysis is like a physician who nods her head as you relay your symptoms while she's preoccupied with what she's going to have for lunch. The modern Devil's Advocacy discussed in this book has nothing to do with role-playing.

Even when a person's authenticity isn't known, effective and useful dissent can still be provided. Defense lawyers, for example, typically don't know the actual guilt of their clients when they argue their clients' cases.[111,112] When successful, these lawyers create reasonable doubt in a judge or jury who have no way of knowing the lawyer's authenticity regarding his case relative to his internal beliefs about his client's guilt.[113] You may view the creation of a counter position based on premises that you may not personally believe as unseemly and cynical. However, our adversarial legal system requires staunch counter positions to enable a vital critical examination of facts and claims before a judgment is rendered. Remember, too, that Devil's Advocacy at its origin was intended to operate like a legal trial.

Modern Devil's Advocates may require specific domain expertise, depending upon the position that they will challenge. For example, in a company that is developing a new drug, experience and knowledge in pharmaceutical science are necessary if the position that will be challenged is scientific. Likewise, issues related to marketing and selling the new drug would need those who are familiar with the rules of marketing and selling in the regulated drug industry. In some instances, challenges can be conducted by so-called *Red Teams* that are composed of members who possess specific subject matter aptitude. In other instances, a lone modern Devil's Advocate without specific expertise can quickly create a useful counter position by herself or with input from those with expertise that she lacks.[114,115]

Modern Devil's Advocacy has been suggested for various policy decisions while acknowledging the challenges that modern Devil's Advocates will encounter. In the article, *Want to Avoid the Next Pandemic? Hire a Devil's Advocate*, the author observed (italics are mine):

> Governments and companies knew about the risk of a pandemic, but they did too little. To prevent the next one, *they need designated devil's advocates* on the state payroll … The problem is: Who's going to point out that the seemingly sensible strategy won't work? In most organizations, that person is a self-appointed devil's advocate, *whom everybody dislikes because he or she sees the gaps in everyone else's ideas or decisions.*[116]

Of course, the fact that a modern Devil's Advocate may face stiff opposition does not mean that the practice should be avoided. It's also important to know that even those who research the value of Devil's Advocacy acknowledge that "… compared to groups with no counter positions, it [devil's advocacy] can provide benefit."[117] Further, there are real-world examples such as those referenced in the paper *Devil's Advocacy and Dialectical Inquiry: Antidotes to Groupthink*:

> Numerous organizations use some form of devil's advocacy. For example, Royal Dutch Petroleum regularly uses a devil's advocacy approach. Before making a major decision, such as entering a market or building a plant, Anheuser-Busch assigns some group the role of critic with the purpose of uncovering all possible problems with a particular proposal and making a case for each side of the question. IBM has a system that encourages employees to disagree with their bosses. The thinking is that a devil's advocate who challenges the CEO and top management team can help sustain the vitality and performance of the upper echelon of the organization. All of these companies have the same goal: improve organizational performance by institutionalizing dissent.[118]

In another paper entitled *How to Get Good at Disagreeing*, the authors refer to *constructive confrontation* that encourages a regular practice of dissent, "… as a group people need to be able to challenge internal agreements. Often this is more about personal relationships in the group than the issue itself. Groups that are used to disagreeing openly generally handle changes better than groups that focus on agreement."[119] The authors' research suggests that as little as a half-hour per week practice can help improve group communications by enabling dissent and offer a 10-point guide for such weekly practice.

Encouraging regular, thoughtful dissent may understandably create concern for executives and managers who fear that open challenges could lead to chaos across the enterprise. As I discussed earlier, however, organizational dissent occurs naturally, and so, working to embrace opposing voices may help a company avoid quietly disruptive latent and displaced dissent. Rand Fishkin, co-founder, and former CEO of the inbound marketing analytics software company MOZ, has referred to the benefits of *psychological safety*[120] among employees, noting (italics are mine):

> It's this ability to have creative, transparent, *healthy conflict that drives better plans* and better sentiment …When everyone on the team has that same positive excitement and hopefulness, and when they know *it's okay to be openly skeptical or critical*, and that they don't have to hide those feelings or risk their standing with their peers or managers by expressing them, the plans, and the quality of work both improve.[121]

A final example I'll offer on the benefits of modern Devil's Advocacy is from an article on military intelligence entitled *Devil's Advocacy and Cyber Security*.[122] In 1973, after building up forces at the Israeli border in plain sight under the guise of military exercises, Egyptian and Syrian armies nearly overran Israel on the Jewish high holiday of Yom Kippur. Because military and political leaders at the time believed such an attack was not possible, they discounted warnings from dissenting voices of the impending attack. The Israeli Military Intelligence Directorate established the Devil's Advocacy Unit after the Yom Kippur War to improve its national intelligence assessments and to avoid future surprises. The authors relate an incident in 2006 when an Israeli naval vessel sailing off the coast of Lebanon was hit by a missile launched by an adversary. The Israeli vessel had not switched on its missile defense system because it was widely believed that the adversary did not have the weapons capabilities to mount an effective missile strike. Apparently, a modern Devil's Advocate warned that the adversary likely did have the required missiles, but those warnings were ignored—akin to the dismissal of warnings prior to the start of the Yom Kippur War, 33 years earlier! The authors, however, note the benefits that modern Devil's Advocacy can bring to bear *if* the modern Devil's Advocate's contrarian view is seriously considered:

> As a safeguard against group think, the Devil's Advocate has instilled an atmosphere of accountability within the analytical process. Analysts have to argue their analysis and be prepared to deal with critique, making it more difficult for individuals to act as a "single point of failure". Overall, the contradictory stance of the Devil's Advocate has served as a check on organizational tunnel vision. Decision makers can be provided with additional points of view, which reduces information gaps and makes their choices more robust.

In the spirit of modern Devil's Advocacy, I make no claim that modern Devil's Advocates *will always* be effective under all conditions. After all, businesses operate within complex systems that lack the certitude of physical laws of nature. At the same time, examples like those discussed suggest to me that modern Devil's Advocacy can be applied in practical ways that ought to yield more benefits than disbenefits. As philosopher Agnes Callard, PhD, observed:[123]

> … thinking together is riddled with pitfalls, but we can't really claim to live together without doing it. That is why we need devil's advocates: they safeguard group-deliberation from the inside. The devil's advocate defends faith and justice by being *in* the group but not *of* it: by keeping the group divided against itself, she holds a space for truth against the pressure of consensus. A devil's advocate is, for instance, well set up to hunt for as-yet unshared information, since for her the sharing of information is never an attempt to be on the same page as other people … we cannot afford to cynically dismiss "devil's advocacy" as a term of opprobrium. It has to become an honorific.

SECTION II

Applying Modern Devil's Advocacy

In this section of the book, I will suggest how you may apply modern Devil's Advocacy in daily practice, addressing you directly as someone who desires to embrace the role of a modern Devil's Advocate. Remember that unlike conventional processes and best practices, modern Devil's Advocacy does *not* follow a prescribed procedure. There are no rigid steps of a formal process and no *right* or *wrong* way to conduct a challenge analysis by modern Devil's Advocacy. Modern Devil's Advocacy is an attitude and perspective; consequently, you may incorporate conventional analytical methods like those that may have been used by the original decision makers or use nonconventional means to challenge the judgment. It is this absence of dogmatic formal process that enables the modern Devil's Advocate the freedom to step off of paths that the decision makers may have taken and trailblaze quickly and efficiently as required.

A challenge by a modern Devil's Advocate can be made at any time, including after a decision has been made and its execution started. These late-stage efforts may help the client and stakeholders re-evaluate their assumptions and judgments and get a floundering project back on track. Alternately, a challenge later in a project may reveal that stakeholders have succumbed to the sunk-cost fallacy[1] and ought to abandon the project before expending any further effort and resources.

The best time to create a challenge, therefore, is after a decision is made but before that decision is implemented. For example, a client may have decided to develop a new product, believing that doing so will lead to profitable revenues, and wants you to suggest why an investment in time and money to develop the product might not lead to the desired outcome. In this case, your involvement may help the client and stakeholders either address potential weaknesses in judgments or conclude that the decision ought to be abandoned.

Some challenge analyses may involve a lot of exploration by you, while in other cases, you may quickly find a weak link that puts the decision you are challenging in serious doubt. In the preceding new product development example, you may need to analyze a wide variety of materials, including independent market reports, internal processes, launch plans, and so forth. However, if you note that the decision was based heavily on one major assumption, such as how a competitor will respond, then you might be able to uncover activities by the competitor that casts serious doubt on that key assumption and the decision.

I remind you to *not* adopt my guidance as a dogmatic process or precise formula that should be strictly applied in all cases, but rather as activities and behaviors that you may consider and adjust for a given challenge analysis. With this caution in mind, consider the following diagram (Figure 2.1):

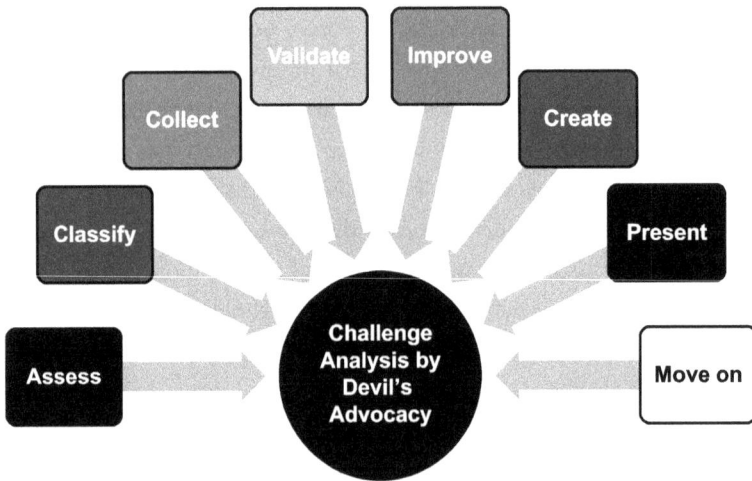

Figure 2.1 Challenge analysis by Devil's Advocacy

The diagram includes eight components of modern Devil's Advocacy. Starting with **Assess** at the left and extending to **Move On** at the right, this arc of activities all contribute to challenge analysis by a modern Devil's Advocate. Note that although the activities will likely proceed in the order shown, they aren't explicitly connected in a stepwise fashion as are prescribed processes. Rather, the Devil's Advocate may find herself conducting these various activities throughout her analysis and right up to the presentation. She may, for example, need to revise her initial assessment as she collects and gains new insights during validation, or elect to revisit her improvement work one last time before finalizing her presentation. Let's take a closer look at each component.

Assess

This component assesses the situation into which you are entering. Your initial impression of a challenge request will very likely be inaccurate. Perhaps the person bringing you in is inadvertently (or intentionally) framing the request in a way that could signal a desired outcome. It's also possible that you are misinterpreting something, possibly because the request sounds like another similar decision that you've challenged. To help ensure you aren't being influenced by a miscommunication or inaccurate understanding, you'll want to challenge your own perception of the situation. Specifically, you will want to identify the true client and to ensure that everyone involved knows what you'll be doing as Devil's Advocate and why.

Identify Your True Client

A client may sit at any level within an organization from the C-Suite to a team member. The internal dynamics because of the client and stakeholders' roles may significantly influence how you will be received and treated during the challenge. The person who is requesting your challenge may be doing so for their own reasons or that person has been instructed by others to arrange a challenge by you. In the first case, the requesting party is your *true client*, whereas in the second instance, the requesting party represents your true client. It is important for you to know for whom the challenge is being conducted in order to establish the expectations with the true client.

For example, a chief executive officer (CEO) may directly ask you to challenge a strategic decision that she is making (e.g., an acquisition, entry into a new market), and the CEO's stakeholders may include parties inside and outside of the enterprise (e.g., vice-president [VP] of marketing, board member, partner, key opinion leader). In this case, your true client is the CEO. Alternately, an authority like the VP of marketing may want an independent challenge of his team's judgments and decisions (e.g., to update or terminate an existing product or service). In this situation, your services may be requested by the VP of marketing indirectly through a marketing manager. The marketing manager would be your primary contact, but the VP of marketing would be your true client.

The type of challenge request (direct and indirect), the true client, and stakeholder composition ought not sway or bias your challenge but rather alert you to the kinds of political issues and group dynamics that you may face. A direct request for a challenge by you might suggest that dissent is honestly desired and welcomed by the client. Of course, direct requests could also be a way to signal to stakeholders that an independent view is being sought, while the expectation is that you will place a stamp of approval on the decision. In all cases, you must mount your best counter case.

As I've discussed in the first section of this book, for challenge analysis to be useful, it must be authentic. You need to be able to mount the strongest possible case against the judgments and decision, or you should decline to conduct the analysis. I accept that, in some cases, maintaining such independence could be very challenging (and possibly a threat to you career advancement and employment). However, taking on the role of Devil's Advocate while kowtowing to the client's predetermined wishes is an affront to the goals of challenge analysis and discredits the reputation of other Devil's Advocates who are investing time and energy to create the very best counter case possible.

The only advice I can offer if you are expected to *play Devil's Advocate* is to restate to the client the requirement for independent and honest analysis and to respectfully decline the role if the client can't give assurance that you will have such freedom in your work.

Confirm the Modern Devil's Advocate Role

If working with a modern Devil's Advocate for the first time, the client and stakeholders may misunderstand the function of modern Devil's

Advocacy and the role of the modern Devil's Advocate. Clients and their stakeholders may wrongly believe that your job is to determine the *right* decision or to simply *tweak* the original decision to put it into a more favorable light. These misunderstandings can start the challenge analysis off on the wrong foot and lead to much wailing and gnashing of teeth later. It is imperative that the client and stakeholders understand the following bullet points at the very start of a challenge analysis. One good way to do this is by a short presentation to the client and stakeholders where you can answer questions that may arise. Key points in the presentation may include:

- The purpose of modern Devil's Advocacy is to create an opposing view to a majority position or decision.
- As a modern Devil's Advocate, you are an independent analyst who will *always* challenge the majority view, even when you might normally agree with the majority view.
- Your challenge is intended show how a decision may be based on weak evidence, questionable assumptions, and dubious judgments.
- Your work as a modern Devil's Advocate is finished when you present your challenge analysis; you have neither the authority nor interest in deciding what the client and stakeholders ought to do.

Although all of the preceding bullet points are important, it may be particularly useful for you to underscore the final point about when your work is finished. What will be done with your challenge analysis is no more your choice than is a prosecutor's option on how a judge will rule in a court of law. Both the client and the stakeholders may be more receptive to your work once they understand that an alternate decision will not be imposed on them by you.

Classify

The classify component is where you will identify the type of decision you are tasked to challenge—what exactly your client wants you to challenge.

Ideally, you'll be challenging a specific decision that is supported by a major-ity of stakeholders. Determining the *decision type* can help you verify if you are dealing with a true majority view or not. The decision type is deter-mined by how the decision that you will challenge was formed and the level of support for the decision as shown in the following diagram (Figure 2.2):

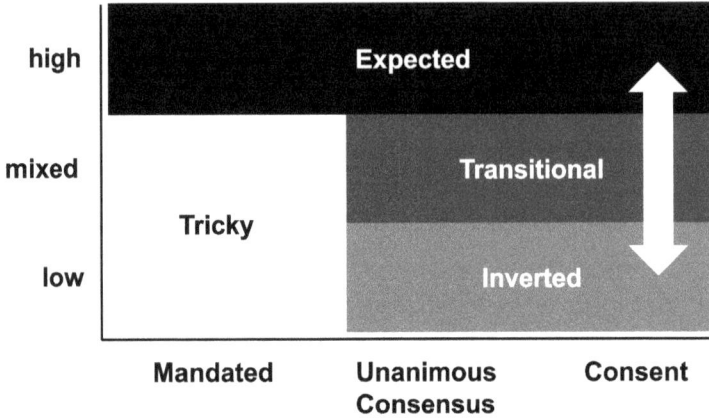

Figure 2.2 Decision type diagram

Along the horizontal axis of the preceding diagram are the three types of decision making that we considered in Section I (mandated, unanimous consensus, and consent). Along the vertical axis are the three levels of support for a decision (high, mixed, and low). Given the three methods of decision making and the three levels of support, there are nine possible combinations. These nine variations can be reduced to just four general decision types that will matter to your challenge: expected, inverted, transitional, and tricky. Although modern Devil's Advocacy can challenge any decision at any time, creating a counter case to a decision for which there is not majority support may offer little value. If the decision type that you are facing is not of a majority view, then you ought to discuss this finding with your client before taking any further actions. Let's take a closer look at the four decision types.

Expected

The rectangle across the top of the decision type diagram includes those decisions for which support is high. Note that it doesn't matter at this point if the decision method was mandated, unanimous consensus, or consent.

However, knowing if the decision to be challenged was mandated may provide you with useful insight into the social or political nature of the environment.

We would expect unanimous consensus decisions to have high stakeholder support because, by definition, all stakeholders agreed to the decision. Such agreement ought to be documented in some way so that you can confirm the claim of unanimity (e.g., meeting notes and project management reports). At the same time, it would not be unusual for some stakeholders to have agreed with the group decision that was made, although they had serious doubts about the quality of evidence and judgments. As with the mandated situation above, you should probe stakeholders to learn if the consensus was truly unanimous and if support has shifted since the original decision. Any stakeholder who may regret their original support in a unanimous consensus can be a useful ally as you build your challenge case.

We would also expect consent decisions to have high support among stakeholders because consent decisions enable decision makers to raise paramount objections and help craft a decision that they can support. Stakeholders ought to have given their consent only after their paramount objections were voiced and addressed. As with the mandated and unanimous situations aforementioned, you should probe stakeholders of consent decisions to uncover strong opposing opinions by those who consented and also to learn if the stakeholders would consent to the decision if they were polled again today.

Unlike unanimous consensus and consent decisions, rapid and mandated decisions may be required due to legal reasons, time and resources constraints, political factors such as public relations, or influence from the board of directors. Consequently, those not included in the decision could be voicing their true support for the decision or simply acknowledging the wishes of the mandating authority. You ought to be alert to any unstated dissent against a mandated decision, which can provide you with potential weak points in the decision.

Inverted

The rectangle at the bottom middle to right of the decision type diagram includes both unanimous consensus and consent decisions for which there is low support from stakeholders. Such situations represent a majority view, but a view that is the *opposite* of the decision you've been asked to challenge! This inversion is completely unexpected based on the definitions of unanimous consensus and consent where the decision makers have either all agreed to the decision or have agreed to support the decision even if they don't believe that it is the best decision. When an inverted decision type is encountered, you'll definitely want to discuss your findings with the client.

Inverted decision types indicate some kind of significant disconnect among the client and stakeholders, or perhaps latent organizational dissent. Rather than continuing with the original challenge, the decision might be restated as an opposing view. For example, the original decision for challenge may have been, "We *will expand* our fresh vegetable line by entering the frozen vegetable market." In this example, you may restate the original decision to, "We *will not expand* our fresh vegetable line by entering the frozen vegetable market." You would then build the best case against *not* expanding into the frozen vegetable market.

Transitional

The rectangle in the middle to right of the decision type diagram includes both unanimous consensus and consent decisions for which there is mixed support. As with the inverted situation aforementioned, mixed support for either a unanimous consensus or consent decision is unexpected due to the way that these decision-making methods are conducted. Mixed support for a consent decision may be more likely than for a unanimous consensus decision, however, because some stakeholders who consented may harbor strong dissenting personal opinions that are on the verge of fervent belief.

As discussed in Section I, organizational dissent can take different forms from outspoken to silent. Mixed support for any decision can be particularly damaging to an organization if dissenting stakeholders are either highly placed in an organization or have strong social connections within the organization. In these situations, the outward appearance may be that the organization is poised to move on a decision, while dissenters are quietly but effectively influencing others and creating obstacles to progress.

Identifying quiet dissent can provide you with rich insights for a strong challenge analysis case. If you learn of specific examples of quiet dissent, then you can try to encourage open discussion with stakeholders by offering the quiet dissent as a hypothetical what-if question. When quiet dissent is openly expressed by you in the form of a question, stakeholders may feel more comfortable discussing the merits of the dissent without appearing as though they were the initiator of the dissenting view or that they are agreeing with the dissenting view.

Note the double-headed arrow in the decision type diagram that bridges the transitional rectangle from expected to inverted types. This arrow indicates that you need to help the client find a way out of a transitional decision type, moving into either the expected or inverted type. Challenging a decision that is supported by half of the stakeholders may reasonably be viewed by the non-supporting half as vindication of their opposition. As I noted earlier, unclear majority positions do not meet the intended purpose or spirit of modern Devil's Advocacy and will likely not be very useful to your client and stakeholders.

Tricky

The rectangle at the left middle to bottom of the decision type diagram includes mandated decisions for which there is either mixed or low support. What makes these decision types significantly different from the inverted and transitional is their mandated origin, and the possibility that you must deliver *bad news* to an authority like a CEO, director, or senior manager. Navigating the emotional responses to a decision challenge can be difficult in any case, but particularly *tricky* when the client sits high within an organization.

In cases where a mandated decision has low support, it would be remarkable if stakeholders openly expressed an opposing view, especially if stakeholders felt that their dissent may lead to punishment or being ostracized from the group. However, such fear may be tempered if there is *distance* between the authority who mandated the decision and the stakeholders. For example, a decision at the corporate headquarters to reduce the workforce in order to lower costs would understandably be unpopular at satellite offices where layoffs may hit the hardest. Similarly, widespread support for a mandated decision may be low if a group like product design issues new brand standards that are contrary to marketers' longstanding and beloved branding. In the first case, the CEO may have mandated the decision, unpleasantly surprising many employees. In the second case, the standards group may have used either unanimous consensus or consent methods, but to those who were not involved in the decision but must comply, it is a mandated decision.

In cases where a mandated situation has mixed support, open dissent may also be unlikely. Not only must dissenters have the confidence in their minority views but must also consider how expressing that dissenting view may negatively impact their ongoing relationship with other team members. The reluctance to openly dissent, however, may diminish if a growing number of people discretely share their views with peers and thereby enable others to speak up (e.g., latent organizational dissent). Your challenge analysis may act as a catalyst that encourages open dissent by publicly raising questions about the decision. As noted under the transitional situation aforementioned, you may be able to tease out quiet dissent by publicly presenting examples as hypothetical questions that provide cover for those who hold dissenting views.

My guidance to you when facing tricky decision types is to proceed as you would do in transitional and inverted situations as discussed earlier while remaining attentive to the different political and social dynamics of a mandate from an authority.

Collect

The collection component is where relevant materials are gathered and organized. Depending upon the time and resources allotted for the challenge analysis, the materials available to you may be very limited or expansive. In some situations, you may be asked to challenge a decision as it has been expressed in minimal artifacts like a short PowerPoint overview or a summary report. In other situations, you may have access to data such as financial statements, project logbooks, and so on. In rare situations, the client may extend an open-door policy to you, so you have access to very sensitive internal information that extends into all corners of the company and the ability to interview any stakeholder or customer you wish. While more information may be beneficial, it is also true that you can be overwhelmed by an avalanche of materials. You will want to try to identify potentially large weaknesses in evidence and judgments that would most effectively challenge the decision and then focus on gaining greater insight about those weaknesses.

You will also be looking beyond objectively verifiable data for the assumptions, beliefs, biases, and fallacies that individual stakeholders may reveal in writing or via interview. In live interviews, the tone of interviewees' verbal responses to questions and their body language may draw your attention in a useful direction. If, for example, you ask the same question to five individuals and only one reacts angrily, then you'll want to explore further not only the reason for the angry reply but also why others didn't seem similarly affected by the question.

I recommend that you always initially interview stakeholders individually in order to avoid crosstalk between members or dominance by any single person. Once the individual interviews are conducted, it may be beneficial to conduct additional group interviews and watch for signs of disagreement and dominant personalities. The first round of interviews is intended to give you a sense of each individual's perspective and characteristics, while the second round is intended to see if and how the group dynamics may have unintentionally biased the original judgments and decision.

A straightforward way for you to manage the collection of information is by a simple chronological list that categorizes the types of information being collected. The typical categories of information may include:

- Date (of entry; historical dates can be entered in the brief description below)
- Source of information (e.g., individual's name and report title)
- Brief description of the information
- Specific claim(s) made in the information
- Claim type (e.g., fact, assumption/opinion, and belief)

In challenge cases that require a quick assessment, a legal tablet and pencil can be sufficient. Jotting down notes per the preceding bullets yields a straightforward chronological accounting as shown in Figure 2.3:

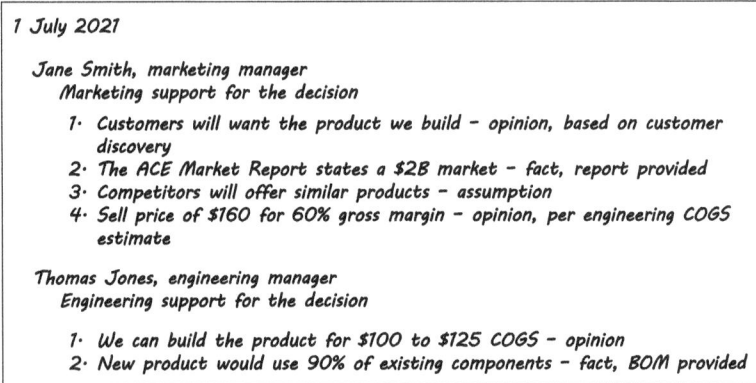

---

1 July 2021

   Jane Smith, marketing manager
     Marketing support for the decision

       1· Customers will want the product we build – opinion, based on customer discovery
       2· The ACE Market Report states a $2B market – fact, report provided
       3· Competitors will offer similar products – assumption
       4· Sell price of $160 for 60% gross margin – opinion, per engineering COGS estimate

   Thomas Jones, engineering manager
     Engineering support for the decision

       1· We can build the product for $100 to $125 COGS – opinion
       2· New product would use 90% of existing components – fact, BOM provided

---

Figure 2.3 Simple written chronological list

At other times, you may have the opportunity to delve more deeply into the analysis, possibly working with many artifacts, stakeholders, and an associate or assistant. In these cases, you may benefit from lists created in Excel, so notes can be sorted and examined to seek further insight (e.g., common claims and confirmed facts). There are various other management tools for diverse information such as OneNote[2] and Roam,[3] but I caution you to keep focused on those key potential weak points that can be exploited rather than to invest a lot of time and effort juggling unnecessary information with a fancy collection tool. The following bulleted definitions are intended to establish a common language for the purpose of the material collection discussion that follows:

- **Claim**: a statement that something is true or is a fact.
- **Fact**: something that is known to have happened or to exist, especially something for which proof exists.
- **Assumption**: something that you accept as true without question or proof.

- **Opinion**: a judgment about someone or something.
- **Belief**: the feeling of being certain that something exists or is true; belief may or may not be based on facts.
- **Bias**: one's subjective perception of reality.
- **Fallacy**: an error in reasoning.

The categorization of claims statements as fact or assumption/opinion or belief may seem unnecessarily fussy. However, as we saw in the discussion of bias and fallacy in Section I, we humans aren't good at completely rational judgments. Consequently, we may honestly feel that our beliefs are justified by strong factual evidence and analytical thinking when they are not. Working to determine if claims are fact-based, assumptions, opinions, or strongly held beliefs can be useful to your challenge.

Claims

Claims are declarative statements that assert a truth or fact; that something *is*, *was*, or *will be*. Such declarative statements express no element of uncertainty and don't specifically suggest that any further examination needs to be taken. A decision to be challenged ought to be in the form of a declarative statement because the decision indicates that some series of actions will be taken (a decision to do nothing is also a declarative statement). Furthermore, many of the supporting premises in support of the decision will likewise be declarative statements. A claim that is made with strong conviction, however, should never be confused with a truthful or fact-based claim.

For example, the claim, "Sales *were* $12 million in July of last year" is not the same as the claim, "Sales *will be* $14 million in July of next year." These two claims are not of similar substance because the first claim states something that has actually occurred and can be validated, while the second claim regards something that may or may not happen. You will be interested in the second kind of claim that expresses certainty where there is little or no evidence for such confidence. Claims that aren't about actual events or outcomes are where you can seek disconfirming evidence and thereby challenge judgments that led to the decision.

Facts

Facts include anything that is known or proved to be true. On the face of this definition, you might expect facts to be easy to recognize and categorize. There are certainly cases where facts are easily identifiable and generally accepted. If, for example, an interviewee states that sales have fallen 5 percent over the past five years, then a review of financial statements would verify that claim. Other claims stated as fact may have once been true, or perhaps were never proved to be true but are widely accepted.

For example, a regional salesperson who closed a large sale at a trade show two years ago may believe that trade shows reliably increase sales, but that salesperson may not know that company sales do not reliably increase after trade show attendance. Furthermore, not all facts are pertinent to the decision that you are challenging. It may be a fact that other companies regularly attend a specific trade show, but that fact does not necessarily support the claim that sales increase after attending that trade shows. It may be a far more important fact that the CEO mandates trade show attendance for other reasons like brand/reputation, whether or not trade show attendance actually increases sales revenues. Facts require some kind of evidence that can be objectively verified, and these facts must be applied reasonably to premises that support a decision.

Assumptions and Opinions

Assumptions are those things we accept without proof as true or as certain to happen. Opinions are the judgments we form about something, possibly based on assumptions and not necessarily fact-based. To keep things simple, I recommend that assumptions and opinions be categorized together (although you may have reason to categorize them separately).

Our assumptions and opinions may be strong or weak, which can affect the ease with which we alter our position in the face of new information. You may wrongly assume that a certain store is open on Sundays and hold the casual opinion that the store in question is the best one of its kind in the city. If you learn that the store is not open on Sundays or that there is a better competitor in town, then you may be disappointed or surprised but willing to adjust your view without much resistance. At other times, you may be reluctant to walk away from assumptions and opinions that you have harbored or expressed over a long time.

In the example of the erroneous store hours assumption aforementioned, you likely don't have a lot of yourself invested, and so, the need for face-saving is low. In other cases, particularly when related to how we view ourselves in the world, the requirement for face-saving can be quite high. When an assumption or opinion becomes passionately sacrosanct, it evolves into a belief.

Beliefs

Belief is the feeling of being certain that something exists or is true. As with assumptions and opinions, beliefs can be fact-based or not. A belief may seem a lot like an assumption or opinion, but an important difference is the personal investment and commitment that one has to one's beliefs.

Belief is commonly associated with religious conviction that is based on core articles of faith. We may adjust our religious belief from a simplistic childhood perspective to a more nuanced one as an adult. For example, an individual may change his concept of angels from humanlike figures with wings, or to simply not think about angels much as an adult. This same individual may easily modify other elements of his faith while maintaining foundational components like the existence of a supreme being and an afterlife. Belief, of course, also exists in our secular lives.

We may believe that our spouse is eternally committed and faithful to us, although we know other apparently happily married couples who have gone the way of divorce, and perhaps have gone through our own divorce. We may believe that our new venture will grow large into a long and successful future, although we know that many businesses barely survive into the near future. We may believe that our processes and best practices will lead us to reliably good decisions, although there is often painfully little objective evidence to support such belief. Identifying claims that seem to be strongly held beliefs may point to particular bias and fallacy that strongly influenced a decision that you are challenging.

Validate

The validate component includes verification of facts and construction of real arguments. As you collect and organize materials for your challenge analysis, you will also attempt determine the veracity of claimed facts and to recategorize them as assumptions, beliefs, or bias/fallacy as may be required. Validation of facts includes checking the accuracy of artifacts such as figures, reports, published articles, and so on. If someone verbally states last year's revenues, then you ought to be able to confirm those figures through official financial statements. If you are given a field report summary, then you ought to be able to get the full report to confirm the summary with the party who created the report and the customer about whom the report was written. The following example from my own experience demonstrates the importance of validation.

I had been asked by an employer to dispute competitors' claims that their lower-cost product performed as well as those that our company produced. It was widely believed in the company that competitive units were not of high quality, based in large part on their lower price point and opinions of internal authorities in engineering and sales. I recommended the simple solution of purchasing competitive units and testing them to confirm their lower performance standards. After we had internal engineering confirmation of the lower performance, we would engage an independent testing group to confirm our findings and then use those impartial findings to educate the customer as to the superior performance and value of our products.

Once the competitive units were in-house, our engineers quickly discovered that the presumably lower-quality products performed rather well, and in at least one case, seemed to have a possible design advantage over the products that we were manufacturing. Although these findings did not provide us with the expected results, it did have a sobering impact on long-held beliefs and assumptions by the business.

The construction of real arguments can help assess the premises and conclusions that we and others believe. If someone tells you that an increase in a product price *will* lead to lower sales, then you can discuss how they are certain of that cause-and-effect relationship. If your question causes the person to acknowledge that an increase in product price *may* lead to lower sales, then you can discuss how they are assessing the likelihood of the cause-and-effect relationship (e.g., very unlikely, somewhat likely, and very likely).

Real arguments can be visualized by a simple diagram like the one shown in Figure 2.4 (which is a horizontal orientation of Figure 1.8), starting with data on the left, that support premises in the middle, which support a conclusion at the right. Note, however, that you will be creating these kinds of argument diagrams from the right to left. You'll first be given or uncover a conclusion (judgment and decision), then identify the various premises that are offered in support the conclusion, then you will drill down through the underlying data. As you conduct these activities, you'll start to see potential weaknesses that you can take advantage of in your analysis. Potential reasoning errors will be found in the premises and potential factual errors will be found in the data behind the premises.

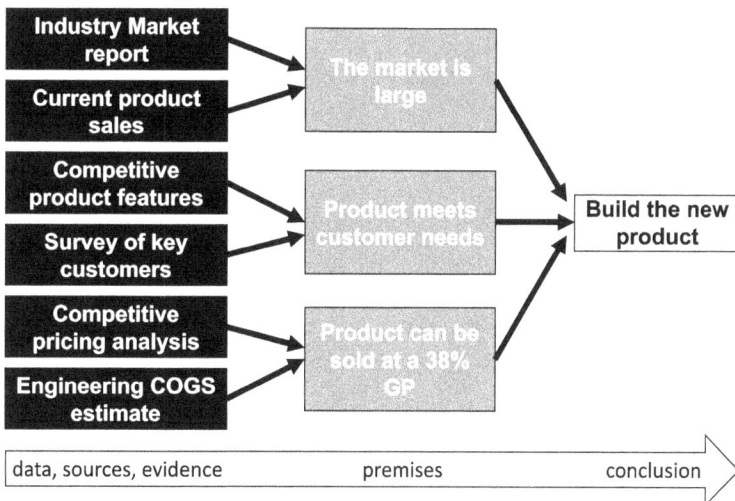

Figure 2.4 Real argument diagram, horizontal

In the preceding example, the decision to build a new product is based on the market size, product solution of customer needs, and an acceptable gross profit. On the surface, these premises may seem to reasonably support the decision; however, the data that support the premises may be weak or nonexistent. Had the argument also included a fourth premise out of left field—that the planets of Jupiter and Saturn were in alignment, then you might understandably question how a planetary alignment would in any way support the decision even if the alignment was factually occurring.

Note that you can create these kinds of simple diagrams by hand or with software tools to help document and analyze the strength of arguments and to share key arguments in your final challenge presentation or report. Your goal in constructing these diagrams is *not* to engage the client and stakeholders in a debate but rather to ensure that you've properly captured the evidence, judgments, and conclusion used in their decision. Once you confirm that the diagram is complete and accurate, you can then step back and start asking yourself questions. How strong is the evidence? What judgments were made in the construction of the premises? Do the premises reasonably relate to the decision? What other plausible premises may be made of the evidence that would go contrary to the decision? How many of the original premises would you need to remove in order for the conclusion/decision to falter?

After you have some ideas about potential weaknesses in the decision, you could circle back to the stakeholders and ask more questions to learn if they had considered other evidence, premises, and conclusions. What other evidence and judgments were initially considered but abandoned, and why? This kind of open-ended, informal question and answer exchange may create a cooperative tone where the stakeholders are essentially *thinking aloud* and usefully reconstructing for you the history of how the decision was reached.

Improve

The improve component is where you will try to support your client's decision in ways that the client may have overlooked. Those who were involved in the original decision likely believe that they have adequately (if not fully) thought through the factors that would lead to a desired outcome. Of course, human bias and erroneous reasoning reinforced by groupthink may conspire to unnecessarily limit the formation of a decision. This collusion of factors, however, does not mean that the original decision doesn't have a lot of merit.

Creating a stronger original decision before you start creating your counter case may help ensure that you aren't casually dismissing well-founded evidence and judgments behind the original decision. By creating the strongest version of the original decision, you are also better able to anticipate where and how the original decision makers may make an impromptu counter-argument during your presentation. You may find among the materials that you collected useful evidence and judgments that were simply overlooked by the original decision makers or perhaps ignored because the information did not conform to the decision makers' perspective.

As you work to strengthen the original decision, you will need to set aside your modern Devil's Advocate's hat and temporarily look for ways to support the original decision makers and their judgments. You are not working to create a different decision or plan of action, but to make the argument for the original decision harder for you to challenge.

Create

The create component is where you will assemble your case against the client's decision. Armed with a strong version of the original decision, you will again review and consider the archival materials and interviews you have collected. You will look for recurring or bold claims, especially those made by individuals who others view as authorities. Those claims and authorities may serve as lynchpins that, if undermined by your challenge, could result in a severe blow to the premises and judgments behind the original decision.

Your exploitation of weaknesses in the original decision is *not* of the minor and inconsequential kind. It's easy to nit-pick on small points or poorly expressed claims, but doing so is lazy, petty, and of little use to the client and stakeholders.[4] You are looking for weaknesses that are not just possible but also plausible. Keep in mind that you are *not* trying to predict the future or to propose a new and better decision, rather you are challenging the decision presented to (and improved by) you.

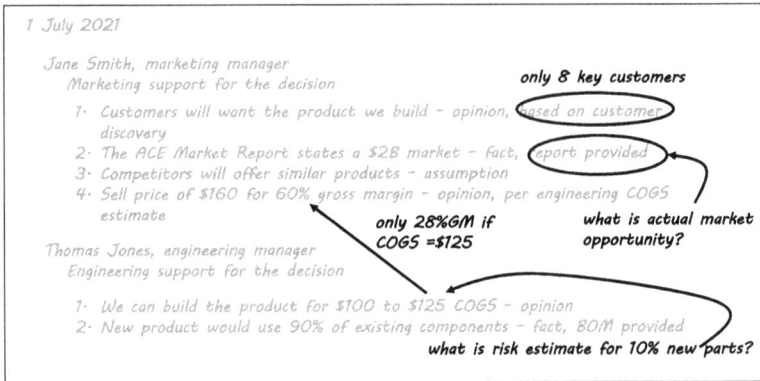

Figure 2.5 Simple notes, redline

Figure 2.5 shows how a modern Devil's Advocate is identifying and considering potentially weak points in an original decision to develop a new product. In the first premise offered by marketing, the modern Devil's Advocate observes that the customer discovery seems to include just a few current key customers. This limited scope may poorly represent the larger market referred to in marketing's second premise, which could result in a much smaller actual opportunity.

In the second premise by engineering, the modern Devil's Advocate is interested to learn about the risk that new required components may introduce. The modern Devil's Advocate links this question about parts risk to engineering's range for cost of goods sold (COGS) in engineering's first premise; specifically, will parts risk increase the COGS? The modern Devil's Advocate then links the potential impact of parts risk, to the engineering high COGS estimates, to marketing's gross margin estimate. If the market for the product and the product profitability is lower than expected, then the decision to proceed with the project may be put into serious doubt.

If you were the modern Devil's Advocate in this simple example, then you would continue to probe a fulsome list of premises that support the original decision in order to identify and link other potential weak points. You would then select those primary claims and judgments that hold the original decision together and create a case that places these claims and judgments into doubt.

Present

The present component is where you will deliver your challenge analysis to the client. As a good lawyer or storyteller does, you will want to present your case in a concise, easily understood, and memorable narrative that persuades your audience. The nature of the final presentation or report will depend on the expectations of the client. Some clients may request a formal written report with footnotes and attachments that they can peruse, and others may want you to just get to the point in a succinct fashion.

My view is that PowerPoint is an ideal tool for modern Devil's Advocacy purposes. It is a ubiquitous tool in businesses, easy to use, offers different elements from tables to drawings, enables you to address an audience in a live presentation and to print out your annotated case for those who may not be able to attend a live presentation. You should take time to create impactful slides that are uncluttered by dense text or complicated graphs. Guidance on how to construct clear slides is available from a variety of public sources such as the book *Storytelling with Data* that I include in *Suggested Reading and Resources*. Alternatively, you may consider working with a professional designer whose layout skills can provide strong visual cues to the spoken narrative that you will deliver in a live presentation, and to your accompanying written narrative.

Your presentation ought to challenge the original decision in a non-threatening way. By this, I mean that your tone ought to be conversational and instructive rather than confrontational and verbose. Of course, you'll need to back up your clean, top-level presentation with key information that you collected and the analyses that you performed. You may benefit from having some of those supporting materials handy as extra slides in a separate PowerPoint document.

If you do use PowerPoint for your presentation, then I recommend that you take advantage of the Notes section to document the simple narrative that you will speak during your live presentations. You will need to know your challenge case cold and won't necessarily refer to the notes during your presentation, but notes can help jog your memory if you need to return to the presentation at a later date. Furthermore, individual PowerPoint slides can be exported in PDF format with their corresponding notes, so those who did not attend a live presentation will have an informative transcript with the slides. Just make sure that your narrative in the Notes section are clear and appropriate for the intended audience (Figure 2.6).

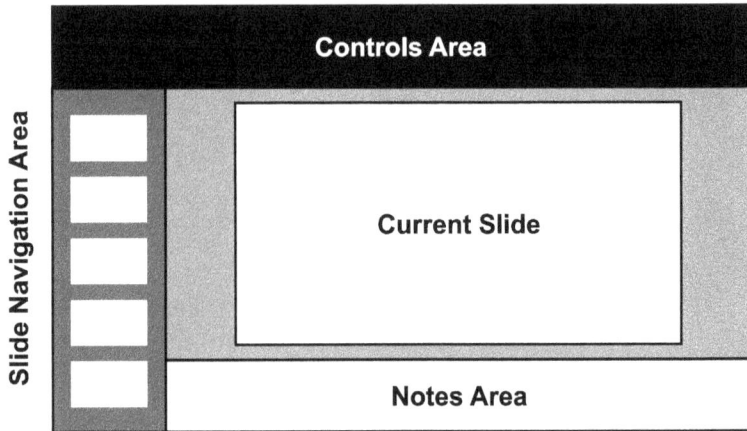

Figure 2.6 Powerpoint notes area

The flow of your presentation may vary, depending on the primary audience. If, for example, your audience includes the CEO and other executives, then you might want to state the key points of your challenge right up front and then work your way down key details as attendees ask questions. Executives are often pressed for time, may not have the interest in *getting into the weeds* of the analysis, and may spend the time that they do have firing off questions or debating points with their attending staff. This presentation you make to executives, however, may not be as effective when communicating your case to an audience that primarily includes the original decision makers.

Those involved in the original decision likely also organized and analyzed the evidence, so they can be particularly protective of their judgments and ready to strongly defend the original decision. When presenting to the original decision makers, the tone and order of your slides may be of a more technical or analytical nature. For example, the first slides could restate the original decision and the premises on which the decision was based to help confirm for the audience that you understand their reasons behind the original decision. The next slides could then state your key reasons for doubt, including the reasonableness of the premises to the argument and the weight of the data behind the premises.

Regardless your audience, you may need to help guide the participants away from side quarrels and keep everyone focused on those potential weaknesses that your analysis reveals. You may find yourself being confronted directly and needing to take a step back to remind the audience that your role is not to replace their decision but to challenge what you believe are important weaknesses. You may be asked to clarify your observations; however, you should never engage in a debate with the participants where you are defending your challenge analysis as an alternate decision—proposing an alternate decision is *not* your role as a modern Devil's Advocate.

After you complete your presentation, then the client and other stakeholders can debate at length what (if anything) they ought to do with your analysis. The client can call you back if there are further clarifying questions to ask you; however, you should refrain from discussions with individuals who may approach you after the presentation wanting to further defend the original decision or explain why your analysis is wrong. Note that your analysis will have its own weaknesses, but weighing those weaknesses against the strengths of your analysis relative to the original decision is the responsibility of the client, not you.

One of the challenges that you will likely face at some point is communicating with authority figures. The original Devil's Advocates were put in opposition to the Pope and other high-ranking officials in the Church and community who desired a certain outcome. Likewise, you may find yourself challenging a decision that's favored by a CEO, senior manager, or other influential party.

Executives who may normally be open to frank feedback can become far less receptive when fatigued or distracted, under pressure that they apply to themselves, or demands that are placed on them from others who they serve (e.g., board members and shareholders). Furthermore, executives understand that their decisions can lead to very poor outcomes like bankruptcy, the loss of jobs, and suffering by individuals and communities. These burdens can create a tendency for an executive to be wary of any activity that may seem to jeopardize their vision, goals, position, and authority. At the same time, you must speak truth to power if you are to provide benefit to your client and stakeholders.

Taking a calm approach when dealing with authority figures may help mitigate volatile, emotional responses in those who you hope to help. Negotiation and communications consultant Holly Weeks observed that when dealing with figures of authority, "You want to show respect to the person while maintaining your own self-respect."[5] Following is Weeks' further advice that may be helpful when communicating with authority figures (Table 2.1).

Table 2.1 Communicating with authority figures

Do...	Don't...
• Explain that you have a different opinion and ask to voice your view • Restate the executive's point of view or decision so that it's clear that you understand it • Speak slowly—talking in an even tone calms you and the other person down	• Assume that disagreeing is going to damage your relationship or career—the consequences are often less dramatic than we think • State your opinions as facts; simply express your point of view and be open to dialogue • Use judgment words, such as *hasty*, *foolish*, or *wrong*, that might upset or incite others

Move On

After you've presented your case, others will decide what action (if any) will be taken, not you! As a diligent modern Devil's Advocate, you've invested your time and effort to create a strong challenge analysis, and it's only natural that you would want to receive recognition for a job well done. Authority figures can, of course, simply ignore your challenge and mandate the decision that they desire. Understandably, you may experience bewilderment, regret, or other negative emotions if others disparage or derisively dismiss your case.

Take heart by recalling other dissenting voices that were ignored such as those who warned MacArthur of the Japanese attack, challenged Theranos's claims, and raised alerts about the impending Yom Kippur War. To ready yourself for whatever response results after you present your challenge, I recommend that you reflect on an observation made by the Greek Stoic philosopher Epictetus (italics are mine):

> Some things are in our control and others not. Things in our control are opinion, pursuit, desire, aversion, and, in a word, *whatever are our own actions*. Things not in our control are body, property, reputation, command, and, in one word, *whatever are not our own actions*.

You have little to no control over how others respond to your analysis, but that fact shouldn't stop you from the earnest practice of modern Devil's Advocacy.

Modern Devil's Advocacy in Action

To put the practice of modern Devil's Advocacy into a practical context, I wanted to offer a real-world example of modern Devil's Advocacy in action. Unfortunately, exposing actual cases of challenge analysis can be extraordinarily difficult because companies typically keep their internal deliberations out of public view for a variety of reasons:

- Companies consider their internal decision-making methods and project outcomes as proprietary and so are unwilling to share any insights.
- Businesses management can be especially sensitive when a decision that was approved by them may have led to an undesirable outcome or failure.
- Former employees and consultants are unable to share their decision-making experiences due to a formal nondisclosure agreement or unwilling to share out of professional ethics.
- The decision-making examples that are available in published articles and popular books are often those that are favorable to and approved by a company and so may lack objectivity.

So, the example that I'm offering next is based on my experience as a mentor in the National Science Foundation (NSF) Innovation Corps

(I-Corps™) Program. I don't recall seeing the title of Devil's Advocate used officially anywhere by the I-Corps Program, but as a mentor in the program, I've observed how coaches and mentors unofficially act as modern Devil's Advocates. Further, because many people have participated in the program, you can conduct a web search to find published written articles and videos by participants (see https://bit.ly/3fl2S96). You can also reach out to I-Corps participants directly via their online presence and learn about their experiences firsthand (e.g., LinkedIn and https://bit.ly/3cuGBDQ). Yes, this kind of investigation would take time and effort on your part, but I propose that your ability to independently judge modern Devil's Advocacy practice through the experiences of many I-Corps participants is better than taking the word of any one pundit, including me!

The I-Corp Program

Created in 2011, the NSF I-Corps Program is intended to "train faculty, students and other researchers in innovation and entrepreneurship skills, to encourage collaboration between academia and industry, and to stimulate the translation of fundamental research to the marketplace."[6] The program "uses experiential education to help researchers gain valuable insight into entrepreneurship, starting a business or industry requirements and challenges."[7] NSF I-Corps teams typically comprise three members:

- **Technical lead (TL)**, typically a university faculty member, senior research scientist, or postdoctoral scholar with deep and direct technical expertise in the actual core technology about which the I-Corps team is exploring commercial potential
- **Entrepreneurial lead (EL)**, typically a postdoctoral researcher or graduate student committed to understanding the commercial applicability of the technology
- **Team mentor (TM)**, typically an experienced entrepreneur with experience in transitioning technology

Based on Stanford University's Lean Launchpad course,[8] I-Corps partners with VentureWell[9] to deliver an accelerated version of the Stanford course. The approach taken in the program is presented as a kind of trailing process, although the participants are very often trailblazing. So, by examining the I-Corps experience, we can see the transition between the trailing process and trailblazing activities hemispheres discussed earlier.

The program encourages participants to critically and deeply explore the pros and cons of a concept through the eyes of potential customers. One particularly important benefit of the program is that participants may have a better chance of success through customer discovery rather than relying solely on their gut instincts, mortgaging their homes, destroying their marriages, and ending up in a very bad place. I refer to the I-Corps Program as a useful *live simulation* of a business startup, and the program has had a significant impact on the lives of many participants. According to a recent report by I-Corps, "Since its 2011 inception, NSF I-Corps has trained 1,315 I-Corps teams with a total of 3,745 people. Following I-Corps training, I-Corps teams have raised $301 million in funding to support startup development and created 644 startups with potential societal impact."[10,11]

The example that follows is a composite narrative, created from my experience as a mentor in both a local I-Corps Program and in the rigorous national VentureWell accelerated program. The resulting story reflects my observations of several I-Corps teams that participated and not just to teams that I mentored. I've organized the example into a beginning, middle, and end in an effort to show the arc of participant development during the program, and I note how the principles of modern Devil's Advocacy are informally applied by coaches and team mentors.

The Beginning

The beginning opens on day one of the program and continues through the first couple of weeks. Participants in the program typically have little to no commercial experience (except for the coaches and TM). The TL is generally an expert with lot of arcane knowledge in a technology domain, teaches and publishes papers, and is a key opinion leader. The TL also often has the characteristics of an inventor with strong belief in the importance and value of an idea that the team will pursue during the program.

The TL is supported by one or two students (an EL or two co-ELs) who are on their way to professional status in a technology domain. The ELs are confidently behind the TL's vision because of the TL's expertise and status as an educator and researcher. As noted in Section I, the ELs' training in science may also make them less likely to challenge the TLs perspective and thereby more susceptible to cognitive bias and fallacious reasoning.

The TL and ELs are trained in the program process by experienced coaches, and further assisted by a TM with commercial experience who provides hands-on support to the team during the program. This starting condition is common in many startups where a small group of individuals, driven by the perspective of a founder, either seek out or encounter individuals who can help them find a path to success.

In the beginning, the TL has what he believes is a clear vision about the features and benefits of his favored idea that he's been researching for many months or years. This vision is supported by supreme confidence that the idea is the *better mousetrap* to an important problem that many people will happily pay to solve.

The TL also has some basic form of protype that can be shared with others, although, often, the TL is reluctant to show his idea until the patent process is started for fear that others may misappropriate the concept.[12] Referred to as a minimally viable product (MVP), the prototype *makes real* for others the idea that the TL is pursuing. The MVP is intended to reveal sufficient detail so a potential customer can understand what it does and how it may address a problem that the customer is desperate to solve. In the case of a digital product like a software platform or app, the prototype may be little more than a dummy web page or a series of images on a smartphone. A physical prototype may be a simple 3D model or a barely functional device that isn't operationally reliable and can't be easily or economically produced.

A core concept in the program is to get out of the office; that is, to speak and meet with potential customers to learn what problems they face and for which they would welcome a practical solution. The lean launch approach incorporated in the program is intended to help ensure that a real and significant customer problem has been identified before investing a lot of time and money building a solution that few will buy. If a solution can be developed by the team to address a problem that many potential customers express, then the team may have a better chance of launching their solution into a waiting market of eager customers.

The team conducts customer discovery by interviewing customers in the customer's setting, and the national program sets a target of 100 interviews (during COVID-19, teams in the national program conducted their interviews primarily via Web meetings and phone calls). The program coaches and training materials instruct the participants to avoid *selling* their idea and rather take an open-ended questioning approach.

In my team, for example, an opening statement revealed simply that we were looking at knee injuries and wanted to learn about the interviewee's experiences with knee injuries.[13] Initially, the TL and ELs were of the opinion that anyone with knees would be the customer, an opinion that would indicate an enormous potential market (i.e., a couple hundred million adults in the United States, the majority of whom have two knees). The coaches directed the ELs to choose just one type of customer who the ELs felt would be the primary buyer, and the team decided on parents with children in sports. This seemed a reasonable decision because knee injuries in young athletes are widespread, can create advanced joint problems later in life, and are particularly common among female athletes. Customer interviews, however, very quickly revealed that parents of young athletes were generally unaware of these knee injury issues and felt that an occasional injury was just part of being an athlete. Note that this finding does *not* mean that knee injuries in child athletes isn't a significant problem or that a successful product couldn't be created for use by teen athletes. However, it may take a lot of time, effort, and money to first educate parents of child athletes before any significant product sales are made. The finding raised the question, who already sees knee injuries as a significant problem and therefore may be ready and willing to buy a solution that the team creates?

Modern Devil's Advocate Activities at the Beginning

As a TM (and *de facto* modern Devil's Advocate), the early activities discussed earlier are partly determined by the design of the program.

- *True client.* The program requires that each team includes a TM member who will constructively guide and challenge the team during the program. The true client for this challenge analysis is the program (represented by the coaches) and not the TL or ELs.
- *Decision type.* The original decision for challenge is the TL's belief that his technology idea solves an important problem. The TL essentially mandates the decision to pursue his technology, and because the ELs support the TL's vision, the decision type is of the expected kind.
- *Collection and organization of materials.* The TL has a variety of materials that are available to the TM, often including published research articles on the technology. The program provides tools to help guide the participants in lean launch methods, including training videos and a one-page diagram called the *Business Model Canvas.*[14] Those in the VentureWell program are provided with an online platform where they are required to share information from interviews, maintain their *Business Model Canvas*, and save their presentations. This platform enables the teams' progress to be monitored by the coaches.

TMs need to quickly gain understanding of the TL's technology and the potential customers for whom the technology will solve a significant problem. TMs will participate in discussions with the TL and ELs, review materials provided, and ask clarifying questions. As I was gaining insight into the technology from the TL's perspective, I was also conducting my own searches on what appeared to be similar concepts that were already in the marketplace.

In addition to the online materials management platform, I created a separate Web-based folder that I used to store and share various materials with my team members. Because e-mail would be a regular means of communication during the program, I also set up filters and tags in my e-mail so that I could more easily find information from exchanges with the team and coaches. Note that it was *not* my goal to become an expert on the technology or to take a leadership position in the team. The TL is the technology subject matter expert, and the ELs are the ones who are leading the interviews and figuring out what next steps to take.

According to NSF I-Corps national program guidelines (italics are mine), TMs are advisors who "… help the team *recognize and reduce confirmation bias* during the customer discovery process. In this role the I-Corps Mentor is in some ways an extension of the I-Corps Teaching Team in helping the team absorb and apply the relevant lessons."[15] TMs, therefore, not only directly challenge the team thinking but also help disrupt groupthink. As a TM and informal modern Devil's Advocate, my role was not to instruct the team on *what* to do, but to help them question how they were interpreting interviewee comments, challenging their assumptions and beliefs, and refining their perspectives.

The Middle

The team continues its training by coaches and program materials and conducts more discussions with potential customers on their way to the goal of 100 interviews. After teams repeatedly encounter interviewees who aren't expressing a need as the TL had originally assumed, coaches direct the teams to select a different customer segment. In the case of our team, the focus shifted from parents of children in athletics, to collegiate and professional athletes, to active military personnel. Every shift in customer type required finding new interviewees through *cold calling* and requests for referrals by interviewees to their associates. Making these kinds of contacts is challenging to professionals and often completely foreign and initially stressful for the ELs and TL.

What the program is attempting to do through this grinding interviewing process is help the team find a practical *product–market fit*. An ideal product–market fit will define a product that will solve a significant problem experienced by a large number of customers. A product–market fit ought to better identify a business that can generate substantial and sustainable sales and profits. Identifying a product–market fit is one of the first efforts pursued through the use of the *Business Model Canvas* (Figure 2.7).

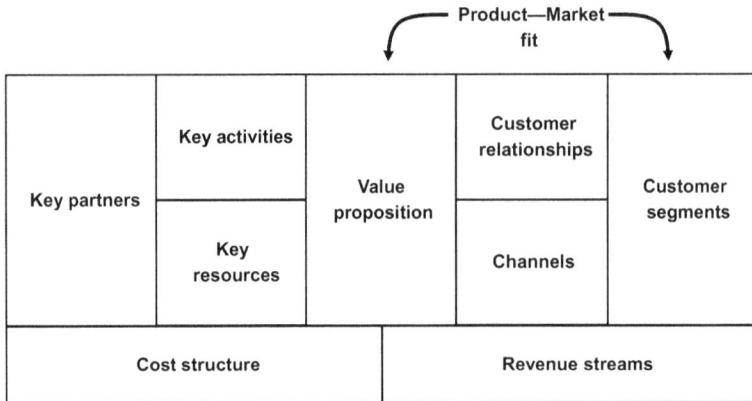

Figure 2.7 Business model canvas

To help find a strong product–market fit, the program incorporates a *scientific method model*[16] analogy that includes hypotheses generation and experimentation. A *hypothesis* is "a tentative assumption made in order to draw out and test its logical or empirical consequences."[17] Scientific hypotheses are typically in the form of an if/then statement where the *if* portion is the independent part that the scientist will control and the *then* portion is the dependent outcome (or prediction) that the scientist will observe. For example, *if* I grow asparagus in darkened conditions, *then* I hypothesize that they will mature into white rather than green plants.[18]

The program trains the team to form a business hypothesis (e.g., parents of student athletes have a significant problem with their child's knee injuries), and then conduct experiments to confirm or refute their hypotheses (e.g., interviews with parents of student athletes revealed that parents don't consider knee injuries a significant problem). Given that many TLs and ELs are intimately familiar with the scientific method, this approach naturally resonates with them. Extending the scientific model method to business situations, however, can create the false impression that the method is as reliable in business as in the physical sciences.

Achieving reproducible and objective proof in the controlled setting of a laboratory is not the same task as is testing out a hypothesis in the business world. However, just as a conventional scientific theory evolves from repetitive hypotheses refinement through experimentation over time, the team learns and strengthens a practical business proposition by incorporating customer discovery insights from their numerous interviews.

With increasing acceptance, the team loosens their hold on their initial assumptions, opinions, and beliefs. At first, the team may be inclined to argue that interviewees just don't understand the benefits that the solution would offer them—which may be true, and very frustrating for the team. As the number of total interviews increases and interviewees begin to express a common set of needs, however, the TL and ELs start to behave more like modern Devil's Advocates. Team members spend more time discussing interviewees' expressed problems rather than in defending the favored technology and initial use case. As the team refines the product–market fit, they also begin training on other aspects of running a successful business, including manufacturing, distribution, and profitable pricing. The coaches and TM continue to guide and challenge the assumptions and beliefs of TL and ELs as they are exposed to these additional topics.

Modern Devil's Advocate Activities in the Middle

During the middle part of the program, the TL and ELs are making new decisions as fresh information is gained; consequently, the TM is regularly creating different challenges. This environment of iterative challenges is different from a conventional effort by a modern Devil's Advocate. In a conventional challenge, the modern Devil's Advocate has identified a specific decision, and the decision type that won't change as she is creating her counter case. In the program, however, the TM must follow the emerging new decisions as the TL and ELs regularly refine their business model.

Early in the middle part of the program, challenges by the coaches and TMs may be met with stiff opposition by the TLs and ELs. Coaches and TMs walk a fine line that doesn't threaten innovation while helping teams confront potential weaknesses in their assumptions and beliefs that can be detrimental to a successful product and venture. Coaches and TMs offer observations and suggestions, but neither the coaches nor the TMs make any decisions for the teams. Taking a more Socratic than scientific approach, coaches and TMs ask questions until a contradiction is exposed, which shows cognitive bias and fallacious reasoning.[19]

In this middle phase, the TM is very focused on helping the team validate facts and consider the strength of real arguments. Argument diagrams as discussed earlier may not necessarily be created and shared with the team; however, the TM benefits the team by constantly considering real arguments and asking the TL and ELs to challenge the quality of evidence, premises, and conclusions. Challenges by coaches and the TMs help create a dynamic environment where the TL and ELs are regularly pushed off balance and encouraged to take a system view where many elements other than the technology must work together to achieve commercial success.

During the middle part of the program, the original vision of the TL and ELs shifts from a favored technology toward problems that potential customers voice without prompting and a solution around which a successful business might be built. Were it not for the challenges made by TMs and coaches, teams may very likely have pursued what they initially believed was a clear path to success, only to find themselves in a startup that was hopelessly lost and rapidly running out of money.

The End

As the program draws to its end, the team is tasked to create a final presentation and short video of lessons they learned during the program.[20] By this time, teams have completed a basic *Business Model Canvas* and have gained some insight about what they will be facing if they decide to continue development, run a startup, and try to sell a solution to the identified customers.

In a conventional challenge analysis, a modern Devil's Advocate would have prepared and presented her case to the original decision by the TL before that decision was executed. In the program, the teams are basically presenting a challenge analysis against their original assumptions, beliefs, and judgments. At this end stage, the participation of the TM and coaches is mostly to review and offer suggestions on how to make a compelling presentation and informative video. For those teams that continue forward, the TM can continue to assist as a modern Devil's Advocate by assessing new information and challenging judgments.

Over the course of the program, the teams get to experience a very small amount of turmoil that occurs in many startups (and in new product development teams within established firms). The pressure to conduct 100 interviews, to propose and test new hypotheses, and to update the *Business Model Canvas* leads to late night discussions and weekends analyzing notes from interviews. Although the experience is a miniscule fraction of the work involved in a real startup, the program offers participants the opportunity to consider if the life of a start-up entrepreneur is really what they want. Some teams continue forward, obtaining the funding and drive a new venture forward, while other teams falter and phase out. Challenges raised by a modern Devil's Advocate during the program help disrupt harmonious groupthink, counter bias, fallacious reasoning, and avoid potentially disastrous outcomes. These same kinds of benefits may be achieved through modern Devil's Advocacy in established businesses and our personal decision making.

Closing Thoughts

We've covered a lot of ground in this book, and at this point, you may be wondering where and how you can start applying modern Devil's Advocacy. As I stated in the Introduction, anyone can be a modern Devil's Advocate—if you practice modern Devil's Advocacy, then you are a modern Devil's Advocate. So, the first step is to commit to practice modern Devil's Advocacy daily, starting with small steps that won't create high risk but can return significant reward.

Start with daily reflection on your own decisions and the motivation behind your judgments. Step away from a decision after you've formed it and come back with fresh eyes that actively seek out different interpretations of the available information. Regularly compare and contrast opposing views on "hot topics" in the public domain like politics, and refrain from dismissing views that don't agree with your world view. Be particularly skeptical about any views that you hold dearly and critically challenge your beliefs. Look past the messenger and dispassionately consider the quality of the many real arguments that you encounter every day, their premises, and supporting evidence. Avoid using the term "Devil's Advocate" in your workplace, rather look for ways to discretely apply the eight components of a challenge analysis discussed above from *assess* to *move on*. View modern Devil's Advocacy as a fluid, ongoing journey that never solidifies into a rote, dogmatic process. I'll offer a final example for you to consider why you will want to develop your skill as a modern Devil's Advocate. Following is the story of a singular dissenting voice that was heeded and consequently avoided an unimaginable catastrophe.

On September 26, 1983, a Soviet duty officer by the name of Stanislav Petrov was alerted when early-warning computer systems indicated that the United States had launched a nuclear missile. Within minutes, the computers reported a total of five Minuteman intercontinental ballistic rockets that were rushing toward the Soviet Union. According to the Soviet protocol at that time (i.e., a formal process), Petrov was to notify his superiors of the American attack. Petrov's superiors would then initiate a hasty retaliatory nuclear strike against the United States.

Amidst a backdrop of urgent alarms and flashing computer confirmation, Petrov anxiously considered the situation. The protocol did not indicate how quickly Petrov should report the warning to his superiors; however, the U.S. missiles were less than 25 minutes from their Soviet targets. Further delay by Petrov could seriously diminish a Soviet response. Petrov understood that if he reported the apparent attack as per his orders, "nobody would have said a word against it."[1] But things just didn't seem right to Petrov.

Petrov wondered why was it that while the Soviet computers indicated high confidence in an actual nuclear strike, Soviet radar was not "seeing" missiles coming over the horizon. It also seemed unlikely to Petrov that the Soviet computers could have identified the U.S. launches and then cleared almost 30 security level checks so quickly. Further, it didn't make sense to Petrov that the United States would start a nuclear war with the Soviet Union with just five missiles from its significant arsenal of nuclear weapons.

True to the definition of modern Devil's Advocacy, Petrov did not follow a prescribed procedure but exercised informed skepticism and stepped off of a predetermined trail that would lead to full-scale nuclear war. Rather than report a certain nuclear strike against the Soviet Union, Petrov advised his superiors that the early-warning system computers had malfunctioned. His superiors heeded Petrov's frank assessment, no Soviet counterstrike was initiated, and 23 minutes later—nothing happened. No blinding mushroom clouds, or vaporized cities, or start of World War III.

In retrospect, Petrov estimated a 50:50 chance that an actual U.S. nuclear missile attack was underway. He attributes his decision to ignore protocol in part to the fact that he was the only officer in his team with a civilian education, whereas his "colleagues were all professional soldiers, they were taught to give and obey orders." Had Petrov not raised his dissenting view, or had his superiors not heeded his insightful appraisal, then you might not be reading this (or any other) book today. What was Petrov's reward immediately following his actions that avoided nuclear war? A reprimand because he did not follow another process to properly make an entry in a logbook.

What makes this story even more remarkable is that Petrov was operating under heightened world tensions created by recent Soviet actions. Just three weeks earlier, a Soviet interceptor jet shot down Korean Air Lines flight 007 "after it crossed into Soviet airspace, killing all 269 people on board," including U.S. House Representative from Georgia, Lawrence McDonald.[2] Apparently, the Soviets confused the commercial Flight 007 with an American reconnaissance aircraft and misinterpreted the flight adjustments by the Korean pilots as evasive maneuvers.[3] Arguably far less challenging than the complex situation that Petrov faced, the Korean Air Lines disaster likely occurred because decision makers who had more time to analyze a nonlethal threat did not think as Petrov had and simply followed orders.

Hopefully, you will never have to make such a quick, life-and-death challenge analysis as did Stanislav Petrov. However, through the daily practice of modern Devil's Advocacy, you may develop your ability to more quickly identify and address troubling inconsistencies that elude formal processes and best practices. If modern Devil's Advocacy is better understood and broadly accepted, then perhaps, better daily decisions can be made in all aspects of our lives.

If you decide to embrace the role of a modern Devil's Advocate, then you ought to expect some scolding or an outright reprimand like Petrov experienced. You will also want to be careful when it comes to personal relationships. I've too often made the mistake of offering a well-intentioned dissenting opinion only to inadvertently offend and cause unnecessary heartache. To avoid such unintended offense, it may be useful to always first ask the other party, are you *sharing* or *seeking*?

In stressful personal situations, we may need to share our feelings or hardships with someone who will patiently listen to us and tell us that they understand even if they disagree with us. Other times, we may be actively seeking an honest critique and frank opinion. By asking the sharing or seeking question upfront, you may be better able to determine if your role in a given situation should be that of modern Devil's Advocate or compassionate *angel*. Just remember that if you *fake* the practice of modern Devil's Advocacy so as to not ruffle any feathers, then you will likely end up reinforcing unfounded assumptions, weak arguments, and poor decisions.

Finally, I welcome any suggestions you may offer for corrections, additions, or improvements to the material. I also invite you to share your dissenting critique about what I've written; I wouldn't expect anything less from modern Devil's Advocates! You can reach me by either of the following links:

- LinkedIn: www.linkedin.com/in/robertkoshinskie/
- E-mail: https://ringbolt.net

Suggested Reading and Resources

Conspiracy Theories and the People Who Believe Them. (2018). Joseph E. Uscinski (editor). Oxford University Press.

Decision Making in a Complex and Uncertain World, free course from The University of Groningen, the Netherlands via FutureLearn. https://bit.ly/3eRTp5K (May 05, 2021).

Exuberant Skepticism. (2010). Paul Kurtz (Author), John R. Shook (Editor). Prometheus.

How to Measure Anything: Finding the Value of "Intangibles" in Business. (2014). Douglas W. Hubbard. Wiley.

In Defense of Troublemakers: The Power of Dissent in Life and Business. (2018). Charlan Nemeth. Basic Books.

Logical and Critical Thinking, free course from The University of Auckland. https://bit.ly/2MAxCDb (May 05, 2021).

Nonsense on Stilts. (2010). Massimo Pigliucci. University of Chicago Press.

ProCon, debate platform. https://procon.org (May 05, 2021).

Red Teaming: How Your Business Can Conquer the Competition by Challenging Everything. (2017). Bryce G. Hoffman. Currency.

Sociocracy 3.0, a body of Creative Commons licensed learning resources, synthesizing ideas from Sociocracy, Agile, and Lean. https://sociocracy30.org/ (May 05, 2021).

Storytelling with Data: A Data Visualization Guide for Business Professionals. (2015). Cole Nussbaumer Knaflic. Wiley Publishing.

Structured Analytic Techniques for Intelligence Analysis. (2010). Richards J. Heuer and Randolph H. Pherson. Sage Publishing.

Superforecasting: The Art and Science of Prediction. (2015). Philip E. Tetlock, Dan Gardner. Random House.

The Halo Effect: ...and the Eight Other Business Delusions That Deceive Managers. (2007). Phil Rosenzweig. Simon and Schuster.

The Hunt for Vulcan: ...And How Albert Einstein Destroyed a Planet, Discovered Relativity, and Deciphered the Universe. (2015). Thomas Levenson. Random House.

The Signal and the Noise: Why So Many Predictions Fail-but Some Don't. (2012). Nate Silver. Penguin Press.

The Systems Thinker, a repository of articles and information available free of charge. https://thesystemsthinker.com/ (May 05, 2021).

The Warning Solution: Intelligent Analysis in the Age of Information Overload. Kristan J. Wheaton. (2001). AFCEA International Press.

Thinking in Bets: Making Smarter Decisions When You Don't Have All the Facts. (2018). Annie Duke. Penguin Group.

Thinking in Systems: A Primer. (2008). Donella H. Meadows. Chelsea Green Publishing.

Warnings: Finding Cassandras to Stop Catastrophes. (2017). Richard A. Clarke and R.P. Eddy. HarperCollins Publishers.

Notes

Description

1. Correll (2021).

Introduction

1. Kenton (2021).

Section I

1. History of the Devil's Advocate (April 24, 2020).
2. Manning (2013).
3. History of the Devil's Advocate (n.d.).
4. Henry and Windsor Fanning (1913).
5. Manning (2013).
6. Heuer and Pherson (2014).
7. Note that unlike Devil's Advocacy both Red Hat and Red Team analysis rely upon more than one analyst, require more resources, and follow prescribed procedures.
8. Groupthink (April 16, 2021).
9. Blagg (2016).
10. Tangirala (2019).
11. Cynic (April 21, 2020).
12. Oksman (June 23, 2020).
13. Skeptic (April 21, 2020).
14. Paul Kurtz (2010).
15. The term, *intuition*, is used here as a form of mystical power and should not be confused with its meaning by researchers such as Gary Klein, PhD, who have proposed that *intuitive decision making* is a kind of pattern recognition that is gained through experience. Experienced firefighters, for example, may quickly form an opinion of impending danger based on experience with many similar situations in the past. As you might expect, the quality and accuracy of such intuitive decision making are contingent upon a variety of factors.
16. Public Company Accounting Oversight Board (April 02, 2021).

17. Murdock (May 13, 2020).
18. Grenier (2010).
19. Shah (2013).
20. Cerullo (2019).
21. Wood et al. (2016).
22. O'Brien (2018).
23. Ramsey (2019).
24. Szoldra (2018).
25. Seetharaman and Glazer (2020).
26. Isaac et al. (2020).
27. Cennimo (2020).
28. Field and Krzyzaniak (March 14, 2020)
29. Broderick (2020).
30. 5WPR Survey Reveals 38% of Beer-Drinking Americans Wouldn't Buy Corona Now (n.d.).
31. Gibson (2020).
32. Schwartz (2020).
33. Johnson (2020).
34. Carey et al. (January 29, 2020).
35. A Report on the Spread of Fake News (2017).
36. Li et al. (2020)
37. Twitter was experimenting with a feature that asked readers to actually read an article before retweeting it, but the results were not yet known when this endnote was included. See Williams (2020).
38. Uscinski (2019).
39. World Economic Forum (April 19, 2019).
40. The Future of Jobs Report (2018).
41. The idea of learning organizations referred to in the Forum Report is not new and has been popularized by others like Peter Senge in his book, *The Fifth Discipline*, which was originally published in 1990.
42. Shah et al. (2012).
43. Lovallo and Sibony (2019).
44. LaPrade et al. (2019).
45. The Global Learner Survey (2019).
46. Gelder (2010).
47. Kienzler and Smith (2003).
48. Senge (2010).
49. An example of a *life decision* is using a condom to avoid contracting a sexually transmitted disease or managing expenses to avoid bankruptcy.
50. Butler et al. (2017).
51. Thomson Atomic Model (April 16, 2020).

52. Korzybski (April 11, 2020).
53. Box (April 11, 2020).
54. *The Institute of General Semantics* (April 22, 2019).
55. Process (February 05, 2020).
56. For a concise but informative discussion about groupthink. Griffin et al. (n.d.).
57. Groupthink (May 08, 2020).
58. Burns (2020).
59. Note that the Kübler–Ross model does offer the benefit of a roadmap to help patients of therapists' understand the emotions that they are experiencing. Any model, however, may limit understanding and options when adopted as a rigid and immutable orthodoxy.
60. Boyne (2013).
61. WHO Surgical Safety Checklist (February 11, 2020).
62. A free introductory course on Six Sigma is offered by Master of Project Academy (March 27, 2020).
63. Wiesenfelder (2010).
64. Show Me the Science—Why Wash Your Hands? (April 20, 2021).
65. An example of equifinality in developmental psychology would be when a girl who is raised in a wealthy and stable family and a boy raised in an impoverished and dysfunctional family both exhibit a shared condition like chronic depression. An example of multifinality may be a case of twin girls who are raised in the same household and only one girl develops an eating disorder.
66. Aggarwal (2013).
67. Maria (2013).
68. Sihvonen and Pajunen (2018).
69. Best practice (February 05, 2020).
70. Structured processes like PRINCE-2 provide for *tailoring*, that is, the option to utilize only those parts of the process that managers deem appropriate for the project at hand. My experience has been that managers quickly turn to tailoring to expedite project completion, bypassing what could be important steps, particularly when the project is behind schedule and the manager is under withering pressure from the C-Suite. Occasionally, someone in the C-Suite mandates tailoring against the opinion of project managers who are still held responsible should failure result.
71. Griffin (1993).
72. Best Practices in Education (April 01, 2020).
73. Pereira and Krippahl (2007).
74. Blank and Newell (February 07, 2020).
75. Canon (February 07, 2020).
76. Blank (February 08, 2020).

77. Determinism (April 11, 2020).

78. Objective metrics and the determination of a sufficient number of instances are difficult to ascertain. Consequently, the threshold parameters are likely unknown, and threshold is a model concept rather than a formulaic expression.

79. Cagle (2019).

80. Maria (April 30, 2021).

81. Tetlock and Gardner.

82. Cognitive Bias (April 30, 2021).

83. Table 7. Survival of private sector establishments by opening year (April 30, 2021).

84. Rosenzwig (2007).

85. Thorndike (1920).

86. Mattera (June 26, 2019).

87. Woods (June 25, 2019).

88. Kruger and Dunning (1999).

89. Resnick (January 31, 2019).

90. Dunning (April 26, 2019).

91. Surowiecki (2005).

92. Understanding Dressing Percentage of Slaughter Cattle (July 13, 2020).

93. Galton (n.d.).

94. It is also possible, of course, that the *experts* rightly guessed the weight of the ox, whereas the *novices* guessed high and low of the actual weight in roughly equal measure. If so, then the novice estimates may have counterbalanced the expert estimates and thereby generated a median value that was close to the actual weight.

95. Lorenz et al. (May 31, 2011).

96. Ball (July 13, 2020).

97. Sutton (2008).

98. Heldal et al. (2020).

99. Senior (2013).

100. Zaini et al. (n.d.).

101. Myers Briggs (n.d.).

102. Winsborough and Chamorro-Premuzic (April 30, 2021).

103. Consent decision making is also known as *formal consensus*, but I avoid using that term to clearly differentiate between consent and unanimous consensus approaches.

104. Sociocracy, A brief history (May 25, 2019).

105. www.sociocracy.info/; https://sociocracy30.org/.

106. Semler (1995).

107. Heuer and Pherson (2014).

108. Nemeth et al. (March 07, 2020).
109. Note that Dr. Nemeth refers to *playing* Devil's Advocate, which frames Devil's Advocacy as an inauthentic and less effective form of dissent relative to those who truly believe in their position. Dr. Nemeth acknowledges, however, that Devil's Advocacy offers benefits when compared to the absence of any challenge—a common situation in the business setting due to groupthink, fear of retribution, and so on. Further, it's not clear to me how the authenticity of dissent is reliability determined inside or outside of the research laboratory setting. I agree that authentic dissent is important and suggest that a *true* modern Devil's Advocate *is* an authentic dissenter.
110. Chinelato (April 26, 2020).
111. Krauss (April 25, 2020).
112. Portman (July 15, 2020).
113. Woodward (2016).
114. Modern Devil's Advocates can certainly seek out the opinion of those who have expertise the advocate lacks.
115. Finkelstein (June 24, 2020).
116. Braw (May 20, 2020).
117. Nemeth (2018).
118. Lunenburg (2012).
119. Brandslet (July 29, 2020).
120. Herway (August 11, 2020).
121. Fishkin (2018).
122. Claver (March 23, 2021).
123. Callard (March 24, 2021).

Section II

1. McRaney (May 03, 2021).
2. OneNote (April 26, 2021).
3. Roam (April 07, 2021).
4. The term *exploit* is used here with its primary meaning.
5. Gallo (May 11, 2020).
6. Innovation Corps (I-Corps™) (Spring 2019).
7. National Science Foundation I-Corps Program (March 24, 2021).
8. Launchpad (March 27, 2021).
9. I-Corps (March 27, 2021).
10. National Science Foundation Innovation Corps (I-Corps™) Biennial Report 2019 (April 08, 2021).
11. It's not yet clear if those who participate in the program achieve results that are significantly better than those who do not participate. The U.S. Bureau

of Labor Statistics, for example, tracks the survival rates of companies after their formation, and historical data indicates that about half of businesses survive five years regardless the business sector or general economy. It will be interesting to see the survival rate for companies formed via the program versus companies formed by other paths. Lacking such a comparison at this time, you may reflect on the discussion about multifinality and equifinality in Section I.

12. Practically speaking, a patent simply provides the patent holder with the grounds to legally defend the idea against infringement.

13. Note that this information is not proprietary and publicly available as a video (June 11, 2021).

14. The Business Model Canvas (June 11, 2021).

15. NSF 18-057: Frequently Asked Questions (FAQs) for I-Corps™ Team Solicitation (March 25, 2021).

16. Scientific Method (March 25, 2021).

17. Hypothesis (March 25, 2021).

18. Harrington (April 29, 2021).

19. The Socratic Method (April 08, 2021).

20. I-Corps Lessons Learned Videos (June 11, 2021).

Closing Thoughts

1. Aksenov (June 11, 2021).

2. McFadden (June 11, 2021).

3. "Korean Air Lines flight 007." (June 11, 2021).

References

2017. "A Report on the Spread of Fake News." *Zignal Labs, Harris Poll.* https://zignallabs.com/blog/fake-news-epidemic/ (accessed May 30, 2020).

"5WPR Survey Reveals 38% of Beer-Drinking Americans Wouldn't Buy Corona Now." *PR Newswire.* www.prnewswire.com/news-releases/5wpr-survey-reveals-38-of-beer-drinking-americans-wouldnt-buy-corona-now-301012225.html (accessed March 14, 2020).

A Free Introductory Course on Six Sigma is Offered by Master of Project Academy. https://masterofproject.com/courses/145916/lectures/11913035 (accessed March 27, 2020).

Aggarwal, V. 2013. "Apple's Biggest Failures." *LiveMint.* www.livemint.com/Leisure/b69npRlXSKUdtF1DV6KFpM/Apples-biggests-failures.html (accessed June 04, 2020).

Aksenov, P. June 11, 2021. "Stanislav Petrov: The Man Who May have Saved the World." *BBC News.* www.bbc.com/news/world-europe-24280831 (accessed June 11, 2021).

"Alfred Korzybski." *Encyclopaedia Britannica.* www.britannica.com/science/general-semantics (accessed April 11, 2020).

Ball, P. July 13, 2021. "'Wisdom of the Crowd': The Myths and Realities." *BBC, Future.* www.bbc.com/future/article/20140708-when-crowd-wisdom-goes-wrong (accessed July 13, 2020).

"Best Practice." *Merriam-Webster.* www.merriam-webster.com/dictionary/best%20practice (accessed February 05, 2020).

"Best Practices in Education." *SERC.* www.bestpracticeswiki.net/view/SERC-Best_Practices_In_Education (accessed April 01, 2020).

Blagg, R. 2016. "The Bystander Effect." *Encyclopædia Britannica.* www.britannica.com/topic/bystander-effect (accessed April 02, 2021).

Blank, S. n.d. "McKinsey's Three Horizons Model Defined Innovation for Years. Here's Why It No Longer Applies." *Harvard Business Review.* https://hbr.org/2019/02/mckinseys-three-horizons-model-defined-innovation-for-years-heres-why-it-no-longer-applies (accessed February 08, 2020).

Blank, S., and P. Newell. 2020. "What Your Innovation Process Should Look Like." *Harvard Business Review,* https://hbr.org/2017/09/what-your-innovation-process-should-look-like (accessed February 07, 2020).

Boyne, W.J. 2013. "The Checklist." *Airforce Magazine.* www.airforcemag.com/article/0813checklist/ (accessed February 11, 2020).

Brandslet, S. "How to Get Good at Disagreeing." *Norwegian SciTech News.* https://norwegianscitechnews.com/2020/07/how-to-get-good-at-disagreeing/ (accessed July 29, 2020).

Braw, E. 2020. "Want to Avoid the Next Pandemic? Hire a Devil's Advocate." *Foreign Policy.* https://foreignpolicy.com/2020/05/06/want-to-avoid-the-next-pandemic-hire-a-devils-advocate/ (accessed May 20, 2020).

Broderick, R. 2020. "QAnon Supporters and Anti-Vaxxers are Spreading A Hoax That Bill Gates Created the Coronavirus." *Buzzfeed News.* www.buzzfeednews.com/article/ryanhatesthis/qanon-supporters-and-anti-vaxxers-are-spreading-a-hoax-that (accessed March 14, 2020).

Burns, L. 2020. "The Rise and Fall of the Five Stages of Grief." *BBC News.* www.bbc.com/news/stories-53267505 (accessed July 04, 2020).

Butler, H., C. Pentoney, and M. Bongc. 2017. "Predicting Real-World Outcomes: Critical Thinking Ability is a Better Predictor of Life Decisions than Intelligence." *Thinking Skills and Creativity*, V25.

Cagle, K. 2019. "The End of Agile." *Forbes.* www.forbes.com/sites/cognitiveworld/2019/08/23/the-end-of-agile/?sh=1274c19d2071 (accessed April 12, 2021).

Callard, A., PhD. n.d. "The Devil's Advocate's Devil's Advocate." *The Point Magazine.* https://thepointmag.com/examined-life/the-devils-advocates-advocate-agnes-callard/ (accessed March 24, 2021).

"Canon." *Merriam-Webster Dictionary.* www.merriam-webster.com/dictionary/canon (accessed February 07, 2020).

Carey, J.M., V. Chi., D. J. Flynn., B. Nyhan, and T. Zeitzoff. January 29, 2020. "The Effects of Corrective Information about Disease Epidemics and Outbreaks: Evidence from Zika and Yellow Fever in Brazil." *Science Advances* 6, no. 5. https://advances.sciencemag.org/content/6/5/eaaw7449/tab-pdf (accessed March 15, 2020).

Cennimo, D.J. 2020. "What is COVID-19?" *Medscape.* www.medscape.com/answers/2500114-197401/what-is-covid-19 (accessed May 22, 2020).

Cerullo, M. 2019. "Influencer Marketing Fraud Will Cost Brands $1.3 Billion in 2019." *CBS News.* www.cbsnews.com/news/influencer-marketing-fraud-costs-companies-1-3-billion/ (accessed July 07, 2020).

Claver, A. n.d. "Devil's Advocacy and Cyber Security." *Institute of Security and Global Affairs.* https://leidensecurityandglobalaffairs.nl/articles/devils-advocacy-and-cyber-security (accessed March 23, 2021).

"Cognitive Bias." *Science Direct.* www.sciencedirect.com/topics/neuroscience/cognitive-bias (accessed April 30, 2021).

Correll, J.T. 2021. "Disaster in the Philippines." *Air Force Magazine.* www.airforcemag.com/article/disaster-in-the-philippines/ (accessed June 07, 2021).

"Cynic." *Merriam-Webster Dictionary.* www.merriam-webster.com/dictionary/cynic (accessed April 21, 2020).

de Carvalho Chinelato, R.S., M.C. Ferreira, F. Valentini, and R. Van den Bosch. 2020. "Construct validity evidence for the individual Authenticity Measure a Work in Brazilian Samples." *Journal of Work and Organizational Psychology.* http://doi.org/10.1016/j.rpto.2015.03 (accessed April 26, 2020).

"Determinism." *Merriam-Webster.* www.merriam-webster.com/dictionary/determinism (accessed April 11, 2020).

Dunning, D. 2019. "We Are All Confident Idiots." *Pacific Standard.* https://psmag.com/social-justice/confident-idiots-92793 (accessed April 26, 2019).

Field, M., and J. Krzyzaniak. n.d. "Why do Politicians Keep Breathing Life into the False Conspiracy Theory that the Coronavirus is a Bioweapon?" *Bulletin of the Atomic Scientists.* https://thebulletin.org/2020/03/why-do-politicians-keep-breathing-life-into-the-false-conspiracy-theory-that-the-coronavirus-is-a-bioweapon/ (accessed March 14, 2020).

Finkelstein, S. n.d. "Don't Be Blinded by Your Own Expertise." *Harvard Business Review.* https://hbr.org/2019/05/dont-be-blinded-by-your-own-expertise (accessed June 24, 2020).

Fishkin, R. 2018. *Lost and Founder: A Painfully Honest Field Guide to the Startup World.* Penguin.

Gallo, A. "How to Disagree with Someone More Powerful than You." *Harvard Business Review.* https://hbr.org/2016/03/how-to-disagree-with-someone-more-powerful-than-you (accessed May 11, 2020).

Galton, F. 1949. "Vox Populi." *Nature* 75, no. 1949, pp. 405–406.

Gelder, T.V. 2010. "Teaching Critical Thinking: Some Lessons from Cognitive Science." *College Teaching* 53, no. 1, pp. 41–46.

"George E. P. Box." *Informs.* www.informs.org/Explore/History-of-O.R.-Excellence/Biographical-Profiles/Box-George-E.-P (accessed April 11, 2020).

Gibson, K. 2020. "Corona Beer Maker Shrugs Off Misinformation on Coronavirus." *CBS News,* www.cbsnews.com/news/corona-beer-virus-misinformation-on-coronavirus/ (accessed March 14, 2020).

Grenier, J.H. 2010. "Appendix B: Sample of Open-Ended Responses." *Encouraging Professional Skepticism in the Industry Specialization Era: A Dual-Process Model and an Experimental Test.* Department of Accountancy: Miami University.

Griffin, A. 1993. "Metrics for Measuring Product Development Cycle Time." *J. Prod Innov Manag,* 10, pp. 112–125.

Griffin, E.M., A. Ledbetter, and G. Sparks. n.d. *A First Look at Communication Theory,* 235–246. New York, NY: McGraw-Hill.

"Groupthink." *Merriam-Webster.* www.merriam-webster.com/dictionary/groupthink (accessed May 08, 2020).

"Groupthink." *Psychology Today.* www.psychologytoday.com/us/basics/groupthink (accessed April 16, 2021).

Harrington, J. 2021. "How to Grow White Asparagus." *SF Gate*. https://homeguides.sfgate.com/grow-white-asparagus-63563.html (accessed April 29, 2021).

Heldal, F., E. Sjøvold, and K. Stålsett. 2020. "Shared Cognition in Intercultural Teams: Collaborating Without Understanding Each Other." *Team Performance Management: An International Journal* 26, nos. 3/4, pp. 211–226.

Henry, W., and S.J. Windsor Fanning. 1913. "Promotor Fidei." *Catholic Encyclopedia*, https://en.wikisource.org/wiki/Catholic_Encyclopedia_(1913)/Promotor_Fidei (accessed April 24, 2020).

Herway, J. "How to Create a Culture of Psychological Safety." *Gallup Workplace*. www.gallup.com/workplace/236198/create-culture-psychological-safety.aspx (accessed August 11, 2020).

Heuer, R., and R. Pherson. 2014. *Structured Analytic Techniques for Intelligence Analysis,* 2nd *Ed.* CQ Press. p. 260.

"History of the Devil's Advocate." *Unam Sanctam Catholicam.* www.unamsanctamcatholicam.com/home/about-us.html (accessed April 24, 2020).

"Hypothesis." *Merriam Webster Dictionary.* www.merriam-webster.com/dictionary/hypothesis (accessed March 25, 2021).

"I-Corps Lessons Learned Videos." *Google Search*. https://bit.ly/3gxSFFo (accessed June 11, 2021).

"I-Corps." *VentureWell*. https://venturewell.org/i-corps/ (accessed March 27, 2021).

"Innovation Corps (I-Corps™)." National Science Foundation. Biennial Report in accordance with Public Law 114–329, American Innovation and Competitiveness Act (AICA) Sec. 601, Spring 2019.

Isaac, M., S. Frenkel, and C. Kang. 2020. "Now More Than Ever, Facebook Is a 'Mark Zuckerberg Production'," *New York Times*. www.nytimes.com/2020/05/16/technology/zuckerberg-facebook-coronavirus.html (accessed May 18, 2020).

Johnson, T. 2020. "Alex Jones is Telling His Viewers that the Toothpaste he Sells Kills Coronavirus." *Media Matters for America*. www.mediamatters.org/coronavirus-covid-19/alex-jones-telling-his-viewers-toothpaste-he-sells-kills-coronavirus (accessed March 14, 2020).

Kenton, W. 2021. "Lean Startup." *Investopedia*. www.investopedia.com/terms/l/lean-startup.asp (accessed April 07, 2021).

Kienzler, D., and F.M. Smith. 2003. "What Our Students Have Taught Us About Critical Thinking." *Journal of Family and Consumer Sciences Education* 21, no. 2.

"Korean Air Lines flight 007." *Encyclopædia Britannica*. www.britannica.com/event/Korean-Air-Lines-flight-007 (accessed June 11, 2021).

Krauss, M.I. 2020. "On Lawyers Defending Views They Don't Believe In." *Forbes*. www.forbes.com/sites/michaelkrauss/2014/03/11/on-lawyers-defending-views-they-dont-believe-in/#60c67c6e2b32 (accessed April 25, 2020).

Kruger, J., and D. Dunning. 1999. "Unskilled and Unaware of It: How Difficulties in Recognizing One's Own Incompetence Lead to Inflated Self-Assessments." *Journal of Personality and Social Psychology* 77, no. 6, pp. 121–134.

Kurtz, P. 2010. "Chapter 17: The New Skepticism, A Statement of Principles." *Exuberant Skepticism*: Prometheus Books.

"Launchpad." *Stanford University*. www.launchpad.stanford.edu/#what-is-launchpad (accessed March 27, 2021).

LaPrade, A., J. Mertens, T. Moore, and A. Wright. 2019. "The Enterprise Guide to Closing the Skills Gap: Strategies for Building and Maintaining a Skilled Workforce." *IBM Institute for Business Value*.

Li, J., and M.W. Wagner. 2020. "When are Readers Likely to Believe a Fact-Check?" *The Brookings Institution*. www.brookings.edu/techstream/when-are-readers-likely-to-believe-a-fact-check/ (accessed May 31, 2020).

Lorenz, J., H. Rauhut, F. Schweitzer, and D. Helbing. May 31, 2011. "How Social Influence Can Undermine the Wisdom of Crowd Effect." *PNAS* 108, no. 22, pp. 9020–9025. https://doi.org/10.1073/pnas.1008636108 (accessed April 30, 2021).

Lovallo, D., and O. Sibony. 2019. "The Case for Behavioral Strategy." *McKinsey Quarterly*, www.mckinsey.com/business-functions/strategy-and-corporate-finance/our-insights/the-case-for-behavioral-strategy (accessed April 20, 2019).

Lunenburg, F.C. 2012. "Devil's Advocacy and Dialectical Inquiry: Antidotes to Groupthink." *International Journal of Scholarly Academic Intellectual Diversity* 14, no. 1.

Manning, K. 2013. "How many Saints are There?" *US Catholic*. www.uscatholic.org/articles/201310/how-many-saints-are-there-28027 (accessed March 21, 2020).

Manning. 2013. "How Many Saints are there?"

Maria, K. 2013. "Equifinality in Project Management Exploring Causal Complexity in Projects." *Systems Research and Behavioral Science*. www.researchgate.net/publication/236260681_Equifinality_in_Project_Management_Exploring_Causal_Complexity_in_Projects (accessed April 02, 2021).

Maria, K. 2021. "Equifinality in Project Management Exploring Causal Complexity in Projects." *Systems Research and Behavioral Science*. https://doi.org/10.1002/sres.2128 (accessed April 30, 2021).

Mattera, S. "3 Steve Ballmer Quotes That Explain Why Microsoft's Mobile Effort Failed." *Motley Fool*. www.fool.com/investing/general/2013/10/12/3-steve-ballmer-quotes-that-explain-why-microsofts.aspx (accessed June 26, 2019).

McFadden, R.D. 2021. "U.S. Says Soviet Downed Korean Airliner; 269 Lost; Reagan Denounces 'Wanton' Act." *The New York Times*. www.nytimes.com/1983/09/02/world/us-says-soviet-downed-korean-airliner-269-lost-reagan-denounces-wanton-act.html (accessed June 11, 2021).

McRaney, D. May 03, 2021. "Sunk Cost Fallacy." *YouAreNotSoSmart.com* https://youarenotsosmart.com/2011/03/25/the-sunk-cost-fallacy/

Murdock, H. 2020. "The Three Key Elements of Professional Scepticism." *MIS Training Institute.* www.misti.co.uk/internal-audit-insights/the-three-key-elements-of-professional-scepticism (accessed May 13, 2020).

"Myers Briggs." www.myersbriggs.org/my-mbti-personality-type/mbti-basics/the-16-mbti-types.htm

"National Science Foundation I-Corps Program." *National Science Foundation.* www.nsf.gov/news/special_reports/i-corps/ (accessed March 24, 2021).

"National Science Foundation Innovation Corps (I-Corps™) Biennial Report 2019." *National Science Foundation.* https://tinyurl.com/b6pj2rxy (accessed April 08, 2021).

Nemeth, C.J. 2018. *In Defense of Troublemakers: The Power of Dissent in Life and Business,* 181. Basic Books.

Nemeth, C.J., J.B. Connell, J.D. Rogers, and K. Brown. "Improving Decision Making by Means of Dissent." *Journal of Applied Social Psychology,* 48–58. http://charlannemeth.com/wp-content/uploads/2017/03/DA1.pdf (accessed March 07, 2020).

Note that this information is not proprietary and publicly available as a video. "2127 Arthrolax Solutions Lessons Learned V2" https://youtu.be/QN7h8ekjfhI (accesed June 11, 2021).

"NSF 18-057: Frequently Asked Questions (FAQs) for I-Corps™ Team Solicitation." National Science Foundation. www.nsf.gov/pubs/2018/nsf18057/nsf18057.jsp#q12 (accessed March 25, 2021).

O'Brien, S.A. 2018. "Elizabeth Holmes Surrounded Theranos with Powerful People." *CNN Business.* https://money.cnn.com/2018/03/15/technology/elizabeth-holmes-theranos/index.html (accessed February 02, 2020).

"OneNote." *Microsoft,* www.microsoft.com/en-us/microsoft-365/onenote/digital-note-taking-app (accessed April 26, 2021).

Oksman, O. June 23, 2020. "Conspiracy Craze: Why 12 Million Americans Believe Alien Lizards Rule Us." *The Guardian.* www.theguardian.com/lifeandstyle/2016/apr/07/conspiracy-theory-paranoia-aliens-illuminati-beyonce-vaccines-cliven-bundy-jfk

Pereira, L., and L. Krippahl. 2007. "On Teaching Critical Thinking to Engineering Students." *Research Gate.* www.researchgate.net/publication/250376476_On_Teaching_Critical_Thinking_to_Engineering_Students (accessed April 30, 2021).

Portman, J. 2020. "Representing a Client the Lawyer Thinks Is Guilty." *Nolo.* www.nolo.com/legal-encyclopedia/representing-client-whom-the-lawyer-thinks-is-guilty.html (accessed July 15, 2020).

"Process." *Merriam-Webster,* www.merriam-webster.com/dictionary/process (accessed February 05, 2020).

Public Company Accounting Oversight Board. n.d. "AS 2401: Consideration of Fraud in a Financial Statement Audit." *Standards.* https://pcaobus.org/oversight/standards/auditing-standards/details/AS2401 (accessed April 02, 2021).

Ramsey, L. 2019. "The Rise and Fall of Theranos." *Business Insider.* www.businessinsider.com/the-history-of-silicon-valley-unicorn-theranos-and-ceo-elizabeth-holmes-2018-5 (accessed February 02, 2020).

Resnick, B. January 31, 2019. "An Expert on Human Blind Spots Gives Advice on HowtoThink." *Vox.* www.vox.com/science-and-health/2019/1/31/18200497/dunning-kruger-effect-explained-trump (accessed April 30, 2019).

"Roam." *Roam Research.* https://roamresearch.com/ (accessed April 07, 2021).

Rosenzwig, P. 2007. *The Halo Effect.* Simon and Schuster.

Schwartz, M.S. 2020. "Missouri Sues Televangelist Jim Bakker for Selling Fake Coronavirus Cure." *NPR.* www.npr.org/2020/03/11/814550474/missouri-sues-televangelist-jim-bakker-for-selling-fake-coronavirus-cure (accessed March 15, 2020).

"Scientific Method." *Encyclopaedia Britannica.* www.britannica.com/science/scientific-method (accessed March 25, 2021).

Seetharaman, D., and E. Glazer. 2020. "Mark Zuckerberg Asserts Control of Facebook, Pushing Aside Dissenters." *Wall Street Journal.* www.wsj.com/articles/mark-zuckerberg-asserts-control-of-facebook-pushing-aside-dissenters-11588106984 (accessed May 18, 2020).

Semler, R. 1995. *Maverick: The Success Story Behind the World's Most Unusual Workplace.* Grand Central Publishing.

Senge, P. 2010. *The Fifth Discipline: The Art & Practice of The Learning Organization.* Random House.

Senior, J. 2013. "In Conversation: Antonin Scalia." *New York Magazine.* https://nymag.com/news/features/antonin-scalia-2013-10/ (accessed April 10, 2020).

Shah, D. 2013. "Skeptics vs. Cynics: Know Which Are Toxic?" *LinkedIn Pulse.* www.linkedin.com/pulse/20130506120216-658789-skeptics-vs-cynics-know-which-are-toxic/ (accessed April 21, 2020).

Shah, S., A. Horne., and J. Capellá. 2012. "Good Data Won't Guarantee Good Decisions." *Harvard Business Review.* https://hbr.org/2012/04/good-data-wont-guarantee-good-decisions (accessed April 19, 2019).

"Show Me the Science—Why Wash Your Hands?" *Centers for Disease Control and Prevention.* www.cdc.gov/handwashing/why-handwashing.html (accessed April 20, 2021).

Sihvonen, A., and K. Pajunen. 2018. "Causal Complexity of New Product Development Processes: A Mechanism Based Approach." *Innovation: Management, Policy and Practice*. https://doi.org/10.1080/14479338.2018.1 513333 (accessed April 02, 2021).

"Skeptic." *Merriam-Webster Dictionary*. www.merriam-webster.com/dictionary/skeptic, (accessed April 21, 2020).

"Sociocracy, A Brief History." *Sociocracy.com*. https://sociocracy30.org/a-brief-history/ (accessed May 25, 2019).

Surowiecki, J. 2005. *The Wisdom of Crowds*. Random House.

Sutton, G.W. 2008. "Review of The Wisdom of Crowds by James Surowiecki." *Journal of Psychology and Christianity*, pp. 372–373.

Szoldra, P. 2018. "Defense Secretary Mattis Has Some Questions to Answer about a Company Just Charged With 'Massive Fraud'." *Task and Purpose*. https://taskandpurpose.com/mattis-theranos-questions (accessed February 02, 2020).

"Table 7. Survival of Private Sector Establishments by Opening Year." *US Bureau of Labor Statistics*. www.bls.gov/bdm/us_age_naics_00_table7.txt (accessed April 30, 2021).

Tangirala, S. 2019. "How the Bystander Effect Keeps You Silent While Problems Fester." *University of Maryland*. www.rhsmith.umd.edu/smithresearch/research/science-open-secrets-work (accessed April 01, 2021).

Tetlock, P.E., and D. Gardner. *Superforecasting: The Art and Science of Prediction*, 92. Random House.

The Institute of General Semantics. www.generalsemantics.org/the-general-semantics-learning-center/alfred-korzybski/ (accessed April 22, 2019).

"The Business Model Canvas." *Strategyzer AG*. www.strategyzer.com/canvas/business-model-canvas (accessed June 11, 2021).

"The Future of Jobs Report 2018." *World Economic Forum*. www.weforum.org/reports/the-future-of-jobs-report-2018 (accessed April 19, 2019).

"The Global Learner Survey, 2019." *Pearson, The Harris Poll*. www.pearson.com/content/dam/global-store/global/resources/Pearson_Global_Learner_Survey_2019.pdf (accessed March 19, 2020).

"The Socratic Method." The University of Chicago Law School. www.law.uchicago.edu/socratic-method (accessed April 08, 2021).

"Thomson Atomic Model." *Encyclopaedia Britannica*. www.britannica.com/science/Thomson-atomic-model (accessed April 16, 2020).

Thorndike, E.L. 1920. "A Constant Error in Psychological Ratings." *Journal of Applied Psychology* 4, no 1, pp. 25–29. https://doi.org/10.1037/h0071663 (accessed April 30, 2021).

"Understanding Dressing Percentage of Slaughter Cattle." *Government of Alberta.* www.alberta.ca/understanding-dressing-percentage-of-slaughter-cattle.aspx (accessed July 13, 2020).

Uscinski, J. 2019. *Conspiracy Theories and the People Who Believe Them*, 20. Oxford University Press.

"WHO Surgical Safety Checklist." *World Health Organization.* www.who.int/patientsafety/safesurgery/checklist/en/ (accessed February 11, 2020).

Wiesenfelder, H. 2010. "Dealing with a Bad DMAIC Project." *Bright Hub Project Management.* www.brighthubpm.com/six-sigma/70254-what-is-a-bad-six-sigma-project/ (accessed March 25, 2020).

Williams, R. 2020. "Twitter Prompts Users to Actually Read Articles before They Retweet Them." *INews.* https://inews.co.uk/news/technology/twitter-retweet-prompt-read-articles-fake-news-trial-443411 (accessed July 07, 2020).

Winsborough, D., and T. Chamorro-Premuzic. 2021 "Great Teams Are About Personalities, Not Just Skills." *Harvard Business Review.* https://hbr.org/2017/01/great-teams-are-about-personalities-not-just-skills (accessed April 30, 2021).

Wood, M., J. Corbett, and M. Flinders. 2016. "Just like us: Everyday celebrity Politicians and the Pursuit of Popularity in an Age of Anti-Politics." *The British Journal of Politics and International Relations* 18, no. 3, pp. 581–598. https://doi.org/10.1177/1369148116632182 (accessed April 02, 2021).

Woods, L. "Warren Buffett's Failures: 15 Investing Mistakes he Regrets." *CNBC Market*, www.cnbc.com/2017/12/15/warren-buffetts-failures-15-investing-mistakes-he-regrets.html (accessed June 25, 2019).

Woodward, K.L. 2016. *Making Saints: How the Catholic Church Determines Who Becomes A Saint, Who Doesn't, and Why.* Touchstone.

World Economic Forum. www.weforum.org/ (accessed April 19, 2019).

www.sociocracy.info/ (accessed April 30, 2021); https://sociocracy30.org/ (accessed April 30, 2021).

Zaini, R.M., M.B. Elmes, O.V. Pavlov, and K. Saeed. n.d. "Organizational Dissent Dynamics: A Conceptual Framework." *Management Communication Quarterly.*

About the Author

Robert Koshinskie is the Principal of Ringbolt Consulting where he helps clients with business analysis and strategy, product marketing, and program management.

Experienced in complex inter-company alliance relationship management, with a degree in Biophysics and an MBA, he moves comfortably among technical, clinical, and business circles, lending his real-life experience to help reduce risks and optimize outcomes. He has co-founded startups and has held a variety of management positions in both small firms and large enterprises, including Philips Healthcare, Laerdal Medical, and Datascope (now Mindray).

Koshinskie shares his experience through various activities, including as a mentor in the National Science Foundation's Innovation Corps (I-Corps™) program, as a certified Ice House Entrepreneurship Program facilitator, and as an instructor through the North Carolina State University Division of Continuing and Professional Education where he conducts a decision-making seminar that he created. You can contact Bob via the following links:

- LinkedIn: www.linkedin.com/in/robertkoshinskie/
- E-mail: https://ringbolt.net/contact/

Index

Note: Page numbers followed by "n" refer to end notes.

OTHER TITLES IN THE ENTREPRENEURSHIP AND SMALL BUSINESS MANAGEMENT COLLECTION

Scott Shane, Case Western University, Editor

- *Dead Fish Don't Swim Upstream* by Silverberg Jay
- *The 8 Superpowers of Successful Entrepreneurs* by Marina Nicholas
- *Founders, Freelancers & Rebels* by Helen Jane Campbell
- *Time Management for Unicorns* by Giulio D'Agostino
- *Zero to $10 Million* by Shane Brett
- *Navigating the New Normal* by Rodd Mann
- *Ethical Business Culture* by Andreas Karaoulanis
- *Blockchain Value* by Olga V. Mack
- *TAP Into Your Potential* by Rick De La Guardia
- *Stop, Change, Grow* by Michael Carter and Karl Shaikh
- *Dynastic Planning* by Walid S. Chiniara
- *From Starting Small to Winning Big* by Shishir Mishra
- *How to Succeed as a Solo Consultant* by Stephen D. Field
- *Native American Entrepreneurs* by Ron P. Sheffield and J. Mark Munoz
- *The Entrepreneurial Adventure* by David James and Oliver James

Concise and Applied Business Books

The Collection listed above is one of 30 business subject collections that Business Expert Press has grown to make BEP a premiere publisher of print and digital books. Our concise and applied books are for...

- Professionals and Practitioners
- Faculty who adopt our books for courses
- Librarians who know that BEP's Digital Libraries are a unique way to offer students ebooks to download, not restricted with any digital rights management
- Executive Training Course Leaders
- Business Seminar Organizers

Business Expert Press books are for anyone who needs to dig deeper on business ideas, goals, and solutions to everyday problems. Whether one print book, one ebook, or buying a digital library of 110 ebooks, we remain the affordable and smart way to be business smart. For more information, please visit www.businessexpertpress.com, or contact sales@businessexpertpress.com.

www.ingramcontent.com/pod-product-compliance
Lightning Source LLC
Chambersburg PA
CBHW061330220326
41599CB00026B/5106